THE MAN WHO INSPIRED GANDHI

PRAEMI M. ROW &
G. PANDRANG ROW

INDIA • SINGAPORE • MALAYSIA

Notion Press

No.8, 3rd Cross Street
CIT Colony, Mylapore
Chennai, Tamil Nadu – 600004

First Published by Notion Press 2021
Copyright © Praemi M. Row & G. Pandrang Row 2021
All Rights Reserved.

ISBN 978-1-64983-958-9

Contents

Contents

Foreword

There are so many people who have helped that need to be acknowledged and thanked.

Praemi M. Row for doing all the research. She, in turn, was encouraged by Shalini B Pandit and Savitri Babulkar. Tara Chandavarkar shared her memories and family lore. Vasanti Chandavarkar loaned *Apostle of Sacrifice* and shared her memories of Gandhiji's visit to Mangalore. N S Kamat provided information on the Ishwarananda institutions in Mangalore. Ajay Row for helping to publish the manuscript. Subban Shiva Rao for his inputs. Mihika Row for her photographs and cover page. Last, and definitely not the least, Satya who helped Praemi M. Row to put down her research on the computer. Many thanks to Mamta S. Shetty and Jyoti for translating newspaper articles and other materials from Kannada to English. Shadiya T M who has helped Praemi M. Row in arranging, typing and feeding into the computer all the information she has been given a hundred times over! Her patience and good nature are phenomenal.

Preface

On a rainy day, looking at some old family photographs, Praemi Row came across an old, faded photograph of one of her great grandfathers, Kudmul Ranga Rao, whom she thought of as Kudmul-pijja. She realized that today, sadly, not many people in the family remembered him or knew about his accomplishments. They did not know how, despite coming from an impoverished background, he was able to bring about a revolutionary change in the thinking and mindset of the people of South Kanara. His actions led to huge changes in that society, impacting the history of the land.

Kudmul Ranga Rao was a predecessor to Dr Ambedkar and Mahatma Gandhi in many ways, although he was not himself a Dalit. Yet, although much has been written about both these leading lights of Indian history, Kudmul-pijja, who devoted his life, and gave up his career and property for the upliftment of the oppressed classes in the pre-Independence era, remains an unsung hero.

Of course, it is not that he is entirely forgotten.

Today, thousands of families belonging to the oppressed classes in Dakshina Kannada and Udupi districts consider Kudmul-pijja their saviour. Sociologists in Mangalore University attribute the wide social acceptance of the oppressed classes in Dakshina Kannada today to his brave efforts in getting these people educated and therefore assimilated.

Recently, in Mangalore – now Mangaluru – various Dalit organisations campaigned successfully to get the town hall renamed Kudmul Ranga Rao Purabhavana.

Further, in a unique double programme, the Dakshina Kannada District Dalit Workers' Welfare Committee, on April 14th, observed the 110th birth anniversary of Ambedkar and simultaneously erected a memorial to Kudmul Ranga Rao in Mangalore.

There are already a few academic biographies of Kudmul Ranga Rao by researchers. However, the writers did not have the advantage Praemi Row has, in that she has been able to draw from the reminisces of her older uncles and aunts, not to mention her mother, and her older cousin Tara Chandavarkar. There are very few letters and other belongings left with the family, so all that is really accessible are memories and oral history. So Praemi Row felt that these memories, which have become virtually family myths and will undoubtedly soon be forgotten, also need to be told and preserved, so that the younger generation will know they have a family history to be proud of and, perhaps, grow to emulate Kudmul Ranga Rao in some way.

All the aunts, uncles, her mother and others referred to Kudmul Ranga Rao as Kudmul-pijja and that is how this biography will refer to him.

ABOUT THE KANARAS AND THE SARASWATS

Chapter 1

Kudmul and the Konkan Coast the Birthplace of Kudmul Ranga Rao

North and South Kanara, which after the reorganization of the states came to be known as Dakshina and Uttara Kanara, occupy a narrow strip of land – about 20 to 120 kilometres wide – spread between the Western Ghats and the Arabian Sea. In the north, it touches Goa and in the south, it extends up to Kerala. It has a very heavy monsoon where the rains batter the land after the monsoon clouds are stopped by the Western Ghats.

It is a beautiful part of the country with its undulating landscape and undisturbed peaceful atmosphere. The green coconut and areca nut palms sway in the breeze blowing in from the sea.

It is also a very fertile land, so it is mostly agricultural, with a few cottage industries providing local employment.

As far as the eye can see, there are only green paddy fields with narrow bunds separating them. Interspersed are trees – swaying coconut palms, tall, straight areca nut palms and any number of fruit trees: mango, cashew nut, jackfruit, breadfruit, sapotas and lemons.

Birds gather in the emerald green rice fields to pick up fish, standing for hours in the warm water.

Wide rivers like the Netravati and the Gururpura and small streams like Gersappe, Basrur, the Honnavar and the Sharavathi flow down from the Western Ghats, creating several picturesque waterfalls. They then wind their way across the land before entering the Arabian Sea. The flowing rivers provide transport and food for the people living on the banks. In the days of Kudmul-pijja, the rivers probably had no bridges and had to be crossed by ferry or, if the river was shallow, swum across.

The location must have also facilitated interactions with people of Europe, the Middle East and the African continent and helped them to enter and become a part of our country.

Kudmul, the birthplace of Kudmul-pijja, can be found in Kasargod district. In those days, it was a small village nestling among the palms and rice fields, bound by the many rivers and streams that flowed through the land.

At the time, Mangalore was the largest town providing educational facilities and job opportunities. It was still very much a village though, and for higher education, an aspiring student had to go to Madras, which was the Mecca for higher education and employment.

At the time of Independence, in 1947, the South and North Kanara regions were a part of the Madras Presidency. It was only much later, with the reorganisation of states in 1956, that the Kannada-speaking areas of South and North Kanara were merged with the erstwhile Mysore State and became the state of Karnataka as we know it. Kasargod, where Kudmul is located, went to Kerala only in 1956 with the reorganization of the states. Mysore State was renamed Karnataka as late as 1973.

The simple and relatively poor people in the region spoke and still speak many languages. This melange of languages and dialects is understood by most of the urban population. The languages include Konkani, Tulu and Malayalam. Konkani is spoken by the Chitrapur Saraswat Brahmins, the Gaud Saraswat Brahmins (GSBs), the Christian communities (both Catholic and Protestant) and the Nawayath who follow Islam. Tulu is spoken by the Bunts, the Poojaris, the Lambanis, the Naiks and a few Brahmins. Malayalam is spoken and understood in the border areas between Karnataka and Kerala. The Jains in the area speak a mixture of Kannada and Tulu. Today, most of the education is in Kannada, the state language, or English.

The calm environment of the coastal region has rubbed off on the people who are peaceful and live in harmony with one another and with nature. There is a harmonious and peaceful intermingling of people of different creeds. Each community has its own language and set of customs and traditions. It is a land where Muslims, Hindus, Christians and Jains have lived side by side for long years without any conflict.

In fact, the coast was known for its communal harmony, except for the brief Moplah troubles in the 1920s during the British Raj. However, that happened further down the coast in Malabar, not actually in the Kanaras. Even this started as a rebellion against the feudal system of the British Raj but degenerated into a communal riot against the Christians and the Hindus.

In fact, it is only in the recent past that communal discord has raised its ugly head. In Bhatkal, supposedly a flashpoint, interestingly, every year, the temple chariot was taken past the mosque where it was blessed by the Mullahji before being pulled through the town.

However, in Kudmul-pijja's time, there was an ugly underbelly to this peaceful existence in the form of several appalling social issues.

Chapter 2
The Saraswat Community

Nestled amidst the trees and rivers are villages in which live the various communities of the area, including the Chitrapur Saraswat Brahmins.

The Saraswats are part of the Hindu community of South and North Kanara. They trace their ancestry to the banks of the Rigvedic Sarasvati River and are supposed to be one of the Pancha Gauda Brahmin communities.

The Saraswats were and still are a small community – in the last census, they were numbered between 22,000 to 25,000, a drop in the Indian population. They are scattered all over the globe, and very few remain in the Kanaras.

The Saraswat Brahmins were mainly agriculturists or 'white-collar' workers like pleaders, village accountants, teachers, lawyers or the like. They lived simple lives. It was by no yardstick a rich community.

There is a charming story, though probably apocryphal, of the time the Saraswats came down south from their original home in Kashmir in the 15th century and settled in different villages of the Kanara region. Apparently, they settled in and around Shimoga, which was ruled by the Nayaka of Keladi, also known as Nayakas of Bednore and Kings of Ikkeri (1499–1763). When the Nayaka asked the Saraswats for their family names, they had to confess they had none. He, therefore, directed them to adopt the name of their village in which they had settled and take that as a family name.

This was the practice they followed. And, today, when you drive through Kanaras, the names of the villages you pass through are all familiar to a Saraswat. For these are the places from where most of our surnames have been derived: Bailur, Bhatkal, Gangolli, Kalyanpur, Kilpadi, Kombadkone, Kundapur, Nyampalli, Trasy … these are all names that are still used in the community.

In 1704, the Saraswats established their own math or spiritual centre at Shirali in North Kanara with a spiritual head. The Swamiji is selected for his spiritual qualities; it is not a dynastic or inherited position.

When the Saraswat Brahmins did have to move away from agriculture, they became a community of white-collar workers.

As Brahmins, the Saraswats of those days lived by specific norms, one of which was a rigid adherence to the caste system. They also followed religious practices exclusive to the community. The Saraswat Brahmins were divided into various territorial endogamous groups, who at one time did not intermarry. According to sociologist Gopa Sabharwal (2006), marriages between Saraswat and non-Saraswat Brahmins were unheard of in the 19th and early 20th century, mainly because the Saraswats ate fish and occasionally meat, while all other Brahmins in that region were vegetarians.

The Saraswats were, for the most part, highly educated even in the 19th century. In fact, literacy was a prized goal. This made them, in many ways, a very forward-looking community.

However, in certain matters, they had an extremely blinkered point of view. Of course, reforms did happen in the community, but they took time. For example, it was only after considerable effort, sacrifice and pain that the women of the Saraswat community were encouraged to study as much as they wished to.

However, for the last so many decades, there has been almost total literacy both among men and women. Being so minuscule in number and not having a city or area of its own, the community has been forced to move all over the country and the world and put roots down wherever jobs and opportunities have taken them.

This is perhaps the reason why an extraordinary number of the community have made names for themselves and made the community proud. As immigrants, they have had to struggle doubly hard to make their lives successful.

The Saraswat community has been fortunate to produce men and women who have been able to make the world a better place. Small and few in number as they are, the community has given birth to many stalwarts who have made a name for themselves in different fields with integrity and dedication. Both Chitrapur Saraswats and Goud Saraswats (GSBs) have given birth to selfless men and women who have risen to eminence for the altruistic work they put in for the welfare of the people, expecting nothing in return. Both North and South Kanara have given birth to many great souls who have tried to make the lives of those in need of help better and more meaningful. They have struggled to make society more democratic and with equal opportunities for all.

The Saraswats who have brought laurels to the community are many. In the field of education are Sir Narayan G. Chandavarkar and his son Sir Vittal Chandavarkar, both of whom became Vice-Chancellors of the University of Bombay; Mrs B Tarabai, who became Principal of Lady Irwin College in New Delhi; Ms Shantabai, Sri Kudmul Ranga Rao's daughter, who helped found

Lady Amritbai Daga College in Nagpur; Vombatkere Pandrang Row, who became the first Indian judge of the Madras High Court before Independence and many more individuals.

The Benegal brothers – Benegal Rama Rau, Benegal Shiva Rau and Benegal Narsing Rau – also are a part of Indian history.

B. Narsing Rau was an Indian civil servant, jurist, diplomat and statesman known for his key role in drafting the Constitution of India.

B. Shiva Rau was a member of the Constituent Assembly of India and an elected representative of the South Kanara constituency in the First Lok Sabha. He was also a correspondent for *The Hindu* and then of the *Manchester Guardian* and a recipient of the civilian honour of the Padma Bhushan.

Finally, Sir Benegal Rama Rau was the fourth Governor of the Reserve Bank of India; he was appointed a Companion of the Order of the Indian Empire (CIE) in 1930. He was knighted in 1939.

From the GSB community, none can forget the contribution made by Tonse Madhavarao Pai and Tonse Ananth Pai who were the pioneers in starting educational institutions in Manipal, now much sought after for education in medicine, hotel management, business management and other disciplines, with education accessible to both men and women. There were two or three banks started in South Kanara, one of which was Canara bank by Anembal Sundar Pai.

Women did not lag far behind in. There were many luminaries among the Saraswat women folk. One name that comes to mind is Kamaladevi Chattopadhyay, who joined the Freedom Movement and even shared a cell with Sarojini Naidu when in jail. After Independence, she nurtured and encouraged the handicraft cottage industries of India, without which a part of our heritage would have been lost.

Another is Mrs Radhabai Subbrayan, who represented India at the Round Table Conference in England in 1930 and became a member of the Upper House of Legislature in 1937.

Another lady Saraswats can be proud of is Mrs Tara Chandavarkar, who was responsible for building the largest architectural firm in South India.

In the field of sports too there have been many achievers. A short list would include Arvind Savur in snooker, Jayant Kalyanpur who represented India in table tennis at the first Asian Games in 1951 and particularly, the unforgettable Prakash Padukone in badminton.

The community has contributed to the defence of the country by joining the Services. Chief of Staff P Kumarmangalam, the grandson of Kudmul Ranga Rao, General B. Mukund Rao, Air Chief Marshal Lakshman Madhav Katre, Lieutenant General Prakash Gokarn, Vice Admiral V.L Koppikar, Major General B Nagesh Rao, Air Vice Marshal Pratap S. Mundkur and Major General Sudhir Vombatkere, who built the world's highest bridge in Ladhak in Khardungla in August 1982 at an altitude of 18,300 feet, are notable personalities.

One cannot omit the Saraswats contribution to arts, theatre, and cinema. Here too, there are some eminent people who have added value in the field of art, such as Gurudutt Padukone, Shyam Benegal, Sushila Rani Patel, Leena Chandavarkar, Deepika Padukone and Amit Masurkar, whose movie *Newton* was chosen to be India's official entry to the Oscars in 2017. Not to be forgotten in the world of photography is Adur Sundar Rao, who was one of the official photographers to the

Nizam of Hyderabad. There have been luminaries in the field of music like Amembel Dinkar, Pandit Dinkar Kaikini, Sudha Kalyanpur and Vidushi N Lalitha Rao.

A very forward-thinking Ganesh Rama Rao Bhatkal, in 1896, started the publishing house of Popular Prakasham, probably the first Saraswat publishing house, which is still going strong today.

Others who must be recalled include some of the dancers who have entertained large audiences, such as Maya Rao, Krishna and Chandrabhaga Ubhayakar. Ram Mohan, B. B. Benegal and Sirur are artists and painters who have made a name for themselves.

As a community, Chitrapur Saraswats were mainly agriculturists and white-collar workers, yet there have been people with business acumen like Nandan Nilekani, one of the founders of Infosys; the industrialist, D.N. Sirur, who took over Minerva Mills in Bangalore and made a success of it and Nalkur Sripad Rao, who started Pest Control of India – he would often jokingly say he was one of the few people who made money swatting flies.

In the field of social service, one of the names that immediately comes to mind is Rao Bahadur S. S Talmaki, who was the first person in Asia to start a cooperative housing society in Bombay, now known as Talmakiwadi.

There is also Karnad Sadashiv Rao, social activist and freedom fighter, after whom Sadashiv Nagar in Bangalore is named.

These are many more names from the Saraswat community that have done the country proud.

Kudmul Ranga Rao, champion of the poor Dalits in the Kanaras, was born into this educated and forward-looking community. Kudmul-pijja realised and felt the pain and indignity of the 'Panchnamas,' 'Mharas' and other so-called 'lower classes.' Although Kudmul-pijja was one of the pioneers when it came to the empowerment of the weaker sections of society, sadly, he is not as well-known as some of the other names from the Saraswat community.

However, his story is worth telling, for he was evidently a man of conscience, accompanied by strong beliefs and great determination, from whom we can learn a lot about courage and conviction.

A SHORT PERSONAL BIOGRAPHY OF KUDMUL-PIJJA AND HIS FAMILY

Chapter 3

Kudmul-Pijja, His Parents and Siblings

Kudmul-pijja was born on the 29th of June 1859 in the small village of Kudmul in Kasargod, a village that is about forty kilometres from Mangalore in the state of Kerala. The area was then part of the former South Kanara district, earlier a part of Madras Presidency in British times.

There are not many people that can speak authoritatively about the way Kudmul-pijja looked or of his mannerisms, because all the family members who knew him are no more. However, what has been passed down tells us that he was a short man, probably 5 feet 4 inches, and weighed around seventy-seven kilos. He had a charming personality with a smiling face and twinkling eyes. He had a tremendous sense of humour; even the people who hated him for moving away from the practices of his community could not help but laugh with him. This would probably have been annoying to other people.

Kudmul is where the Kudmul Saraswat Brahmin family lived. Kudmul-pijja's father, Sri Devappayya, worked as a clerk for a Muslim trader at the port of Mangalore. Devappayya was a simple and religious man who lived a middle-class, albeit bordering on poor, life. Kudmul-pijja's mother, Smt. Gaury, too was a deeply pious and gentle lady, unlettered but true to her husband and family. Kudmul-pijja was the eldest son of seven children. We do not know the names of all his siblings; however, we do know that one brother was named Sadashiv Rao – he never married.

We do not know too much about Kudmul-pijja's family. What we do know is that they were loving and supportive.

We also do not know which parent's influence impressed and guided Kudmul-pijja's young mind and exercised greater influence in the formation of his character – his father or his mother. It was probably his mother because his father died young, while his mother lived to an advanced age and predeceased him only by a few years. Of course, we can't be sure of this.

What is certain, however, is that Kudmul-pijja's character was greatly shaped by the hardships he faced when he lost his father suddenly, when he was still very young.

Kudmul-pijja's father had got him married when he was very young – he was, in fact, just twelve and his wife, Rukmini-amma, was literally a child, just nine years of age. But, in those times this was not considered unusual. For example, one of the older members of the family, Kalyani Ullal, was just seven years old when she got married.

Rukmini-amma was the daughter of the head clerk at the munsiff's court in Kasargod. The post of Head Clerk was considered extremely prestigious in those days, so her father was a man of some standing. It may be interesting to ask why he married his daughter to Kudmul-pijja since he was not yet a matriculate and he came from a relatively poor family with no assets. The only plausible explanation is that Rumini-amma's father saw potential in his son-in-law and felt he would do well in life.

Rukmini-amma was a gentle and loving lady who played an unhesitatingly supportive role in her husband's life. She never said a word against her husband nor interfered in his social, religious and humanitarian activities. She always stood firmly with her husband, although it must have been difficult for her because his ideas and principles were often completely contrary to her own upbringing, not to mention social customs.

At 16, Kudmul-pijja lost his father, who left behind three sons and four daughters, of whom only two were married. The others were yet to be settled and Kudmul-pijja's two younger brothers were still to be educated.

At the time of his death, Sri Devappayya was earning a salary of fifteen rupees a month. In those times, salaries were not necessarily paid at the end of every month but would be written in the ledger against the name of the clerk as being arrears due to him and against his account. The amount due to him, or a portion of it, was actually paid at the time of Deepavali when accounts were closed and the balance was carried forward for the next year.

As was the practice in those days, there were no records kept of income and expenditure. No material is available to show the expenditure in the family. This was more so in poor families where devoting time for earning a salary to support the family was more important than keeping the accounts.

Kudmul-pijja and Rukmini-amma had only been married four years when he was orphaned. Life could not have been easy for the young couple because on the death of his father, Kudmul-pijja became the sole earning member of his family. Rukmini-amma and he had to bear the onus of educating his brothers and making sure his sisters were married and settled. He managed this and his youngest sister was married in 1880.

Chapter 4
Life After His Father's Death

After the death of his father and in straitened circumstances, Kudmul-pijja needed to earn a reasonable amount of money for the family, so he opted for a teacher's job that paid him eight rupees a month. This meant that after Sri Devappayya's passing, the family income came down from fifteen rupees to eight rupees. This could not have been easy for them.

Of course, although eight rupees sounds like a minuscule amount to us today, in that period it was enough to feed a family. We have to keep in mind that a maund of rice (a maund was a measure of weight in British India, which added up to approximately thirty-eight kilos) cost 1.8 annas and rent for a small house was four to eight annas. A rupee was made up of sixteen annas and each anna had twelve pies. This changed when the decimal system of money was introduced into India.

Even so, when Kudmul-pijja lost his father and took up a house on rent, his salary as a teacher meant that he could only afford a hut with a thatched roof. This could not have been comfortable in the Mangalore monsoons and summer. However, Kudmul-pijja was not one to dwell on his problems, so, amid all these hardships, while teaching, he completed his primary education at Kasargod.

As a teacher, Kudmul-pijja became very popular, a mentor to his students as well as a role model. He was reportedly very likeable and down to earth.

From his first job in Kasargod, Kudmul-pijja then moved to become a schoolmaster at the local school in Kaikal, which followed the Board curriculum. After working there for some time, he came to Mangalore and joined a municipal school as one of its teachers.

A teacher in those times was a respected person, was considered a 'guru' and was honoured and loved. Sometimes, when money was scarce, teachers were paid in kind by parents.

Although he worked as a teacher for a few years and was good at his job, Kudmul-pijja had aspirations to study further. He could not pass his matriculation exam at the first attempt due to financial difficulties, but he was determined to study and make a life for himself. So he finally passed his matriculation later through a correspondence course. Kudmul-pijja then obtained a degree from the 147-year-old University College (formerly called Government College) in Mangalore.

This institution was started in 1868 with 315 students as a provincial school and now offers courses at the degree level. It has had a long list of many eminent and distinguished alumni, who are remembered for their contribution in various fields. The list includes eminent personalities like Kannada writer Panje Mangesh Rao; Benegal Rama Rau, former Governor of the Reserve Bank of India; Kamaladev Chattopadya, who revived many of the forgotten ancient arts and crafts of India; Karnad Sadashiv Rao, the freedom fighter and Congressman; Molahalli Shiva Rao, who founded Kanara District Central Cooperative Bank and many others.

Kudmul-pijja seems to have been an unusual person. He was able to persuade people to adopt his extremely advanced ideas. He had a strong will and the determination to fight through every obstacle without hurting anybody. It was difficult to get him to change his mind or reverse any decision he had taken because these decisions would have been made after a great deal of thought and deliberation. He did not abandon his principles on confronting adversity.

Though Kudmul-pijja was a great fighter, he was the most innocent of souls. He was often the victim of fraud and seems to have lacked any sort of guile. He had no secrets and was constitutionally incapable of telling even the most harmless lie.

Kudmul-pijja had a sense of humour. From the following poem that is both touching and humorous, we can see Kudmul-pijja's irreverence and deep faith even in his daily life.

Monday: Wash Day

Shiva, help me wash away all my selfishness and

Vanity, so I may serve you with perfect humility

Through the week ahead.

Tuesday: Ironing Day

Oh Shiva, help me iron out all the wrinkles

Of prejudice, I have collected through the years

So that I may see the beauty in others.

Wednesday: Mending Day

O, Shiva help me mend my ways so I will not

Set a bad example for others.

Thursday: Cleaning Day

Oh Shiva, help me to dust out all the many faults

I have been hiding in the secret corners of my heart

Friday: Shopping day

Oh Shiva, give me the grace to ask wisely so I may purchase

Eternal happiness for myself and all others

In need of love, And accept my pooja

Saturday: Cooking Day

Help me, brew a big kettle of brotherly

Love and serve it with clean, sweet bread of human kindness,

to the needy

Sunday

Oh Shiva, I have prepared my house for you. Please

Come into my heart so I may spend the day and the

Rest of my life in your presence.

Kudmul-pijja also had certain endearing habits, although they must have been annoying for his wife.

One idiosyncrasy was that he never threw anything away. He stored everything in a drawer by his desk – from used matchsticks to pen nibs. His daughter, Lalithabai, used to recall that his drawer was like a magic box containing everything that could be put to use. When he was asked to get rid of things he would ask, "Why? They may come in handy at some time."

Praemi remembers that Lalithabai had the same habit and she used to say, "Don't ask me if I have it; always say, 'please give it to me,' because I will find it for you."

However, Kudmul-pijja was evidently not acquisitive or attached to material things. In 1905, when a friend of his sent him a gold fountain pen from Bombay, he looked at it and immediately gave it to his eldest grandson saying, "I don't need such an expensive pen. Any pen can do the same job."

He was a humble person but at the same time, he was known to lose his temper on occasion.

Once in Daddalkad, a colony in Mangalore, Daddalkad Anand, the son of Babu, popularly known as 'Lame Teacher' Babu, was working in the Depressed Class Mission (DCM) that Kudmul-pijja had founded, as his helper. Anand was supposed to deliver letters daily from the office at Shedigudde and Court Hill School to Kudmul-pijja's house. One day, Kudmul-pijja had to go out early for some important work. He called Anand and requested him to bring the letters before 10 AM the next morning.

But the headmaster of the Shedigudde School on that particular day was late, so Anand was delayed. He hurried but could deliver the letters only after 10.30 AM.

Kudmul-pijja was furious and he twisted Anand's ears even though the young helper folded his hands and tried to tell him what had happened. But Kudmul-pijja was enraged. He did not listen to the young man and sent him away after shouting at him.

The young man narrated the incident to the headmaster. The headmaster, feeling guilty, wrote a letter to Kudmul-pijja, telling him the real story. On learning the truth, Kudmul-pijja, who had the rare ability of being able to admit his mistakes, regretted his hasty actions. To show how sorry he was, every day he would share one idli and a cup of coffee from his breakfast with Anand.

Kudmul-pijja loved reading. This trait seems to have been inherited by his family who all love books and reading.

Kudmul-pijja also wrote well. He wrote short and pithy letters and this too seems to have been passed down. His daughter, Lalitha Bai, inherited this trait as well. She wrote beautiful letters.

A few of his grandchildren seem to have got his genes and a couple of them have published books.

Sometime before he took up *Sanyasa*, he told Lalithabai that he would, one day, write his autobiography but he seems to have changed his mind. Being a modest man, he told those around him that his name should be forgotten and his work remembered. Regretfully, he destroyed most of his correspondence, along with citations and rewards he had received.

Kudmul-pijja never sought out publicity or praise for himself. If at all, it was for the work he was doing.

Once, a rather unexpected event took place, which touched and embarrassed him at the same time.

In Jedigudde, later known as Shedigudde, Udupi Raghvendra, a student from the untouchable community, was studying in the primary class of the DCM. He had great respect and love for his mentor. The young lad, apart from being intelligent, was also a poet. Being poor, he must have felt that the only way to pay his respect to Kudmul-pijja was to write a poem expressing his feelings and showing the gratitude and love that he had for him. He praised and extolled Kudmul-pijja in a verse, which he then presented to him.

On reading the poem, Kudmul-pijja was moved to tears and Raghvendra was scared that he had somehow hurt his teacher. But, Kudmul-pijja first reassured the boy and then he told him that he was not worthy of such praise. He added that what he had done was not as noteworthy as depicted in the poem. He told the boy not to show or read the poem to anyone until after his death.

Kudmul-pijja refused to even sit for a photograph. The family only has a couple of photographs of him and they are grainy and unclear.

After Kudmul-pijja's death, his grandson N. Rama Rao collected whatever was left of his papers, including letters to the great men of the time like Gandhiji, and gave it to his lawyer to sort out and categorise. Unfortunately, the lawyer's wife was illiterate, and looking at these old and dusty papers thought they were to be destroyed, so she sold them to the waste paper-wallah.

So, even the little that would have been available was destroyed, making it difficult for his ancestors to write about him. The family will never know the true workings of his mind, thoughts, triumphs, defeats, pains and frustrations. Even now, over a century later, it would have been a joy to read and enjoy more of those letters, had they been preserved.

Kudmul-pijja had two books that he treasured. One was called *Daily Strength*. It had inspiring extracts from the writings of great persons from the times gone by. This book was presented to his daughter to read from and she, in turn, gave it to her son, N Rama Rao.

The second was a book of bhajans, which was also gifted to Lalithabai to recite from. She gave it to her son, N Rama Rao.

Neither of these books can be traced. Only the cover of the book of bhajans remains with his hand-writing on it.

Chapter 5

Ullal Raghunathaiah, Brother-In-Law, Friend, Inspiration

While Kudmul-pijja was still teaching in school, he came in touch with another extraordinary man who also had ideas far ahead of the times – Ullal Raghunathaiah.

At the time, Kudmul-pijja was completing the process of marrying off his younger siblings. He finally succeeded in marrying his youngest and last sister in 1880 to Ullal Raghunathaiah, whose first wife had died a few months earlier. His parents wanted to find another bride for their son and they chose Kudmul-pijja's sister. Although Raghunathaiah already had children, Kudmul-pijja was not in a position to decline the offer as he did not have much to offer his sisters in the way of worldly goods.

It was a fortuitous choice.

Ullal Raghunathaiah was a remarkable person who stood for the freedom of action and liberty of thought against traditional religion. He and Kudmul-pijja were not just brothers-in-law, they became close friends and fellow activists for the social good.

Many of their common causes changed the face of the Kanaras.

Chapter 6
The Brahmo Samaj

The Brahmo Samaj movement was started by Raja Ram Mohan Roy in Calcutta in 1828. He was completely disillusioned with Hindu practices and the hold that the priestly castes had on their co-religionists. He was a strong believer that certain Hindu practices were cruel and unnecessary and they had to be abolished. He disapproved of customs like child marriage, exploitation of Hindu widows, untouchability, social injustice and the Devadasi system. The Brahmo Samaj was created to address these problems and make a change in Hindu society.

After the death of Raja Ram Mohan Roy, the movement drew inspiration from stalwarts like Ishwar Chandra Vidyasagar, Keshub Chandra Sen and Debendranath Tagore.

Raghunathaiah and Kudmul-pijja also got inspiration from the stalwarts of the Brahmo Samaj movement. As a matter of fact, the ideals and principles of the Brahmo Samaj matched theirs. And they were not alone.

The ideals of the movement appealed to luminaries like Kondegi Deva Rai, Karnad Sadashiva Rao and Bhardwaj Shiv Raj as well.

So, Raghunathaiah and this group of forward-thinking men started the Brahmo Samaj movement in South Kanara. Initial meetings took place in Ullal, a small village on the banks of the Netravati River.

Under Raghunathaiah's influence, Kudmul-pijja developed an interest in the Brahmo Samaj's liberal ideologies, aims and religious activities. He determined that the self-purification of every human being would be the right solution to solve the overwhelming social problems that beset the area.

The tenets of the Brahmo Samaj are likely to have guided Kudmul-pijja to change people's attitudes towards the socials ills existing Kanara. He truly believed in its principles and ideals, so strongly that he became the secretary of the Brahmo Samaj in South Kanara.

Brahmo Samaj members used to meet regularly in Mangalore. Kudmul-pijja was instrumental in encouraging a good many people around him to attend these meetings.

Being a person with a thirst for knowledge, Kudmul-pijja also studied different religions and could give illuminating discourses on them.

Once a week, at the meetings of the Brahmo Samaj, a member would be invited to address the gathering. Generally, members of each faith were asked to talk about their beliefs and religions. They were asked to first study the life and faith of religious leaders like Buddha, Jesus Christ, Chaitanya and Prophet Mohammed and talk about their learnings for an hour at every meeting.

As part of this practice, Kudmul-pijja would give eloquent speeches in Kannada, English, Konkani and Tulu. Being a polyglot, he was fluent in all these languages, which he also wrote well. He believed that it is important to know your mother tongue as well as the local languages of the area.

Kudmul-pijja obviously had a sense of humour. Once, while making a speech, he said, "God has given us eyes to see evil."

Someone from the audience shouted, "Yes and eyelids too!"

This made him laugh out loud.

Prayers were also chanted at the Mission house every Sunday evening.

Before the Brahmo Samaj was recognised as a movement, these meetings were held in secret in somebody's home for fear of ridicule and punishment. To make matters worse, any contact with Raghunathaiah or Kudmul-pijja could incur severe displeasure from the community, including Pandurangashram Swami, the religious head of the Swaraswats, who was against any organisation that questioned his authority.

After the Brahmo Samaj Mandir was built in 1882, all activities were conducted there.

At some point in time, missionaries from Germany had arrived in Mangalore and were preaching Christianity. The influence of these missionaries had an impact on Raghunathaiah and he converted to Catholicism.

This hasty decision hurt the feelings of his family members.

According to the records of Sri Nyampalli Rama Rao, Kudmul-pijja's grandson, after realizing how much pain he was causing, Raghunathaiah turned away from Christianity and joined the Brahmo Samaj once more. No one doubted Raghunathaiah was a devout Hindu, but he was more comfortable with the precepts of the Samaj. The wretched, cruel and discriminatory customs of traditional Hinduism as followed at the time were an anathema to him.

Kudmul-pijja's children too joined the Brahmo Samaj and participated in all the religious ceremonies. Of course, he never forced anything on them. For example, his granddaughters-in-law were Hindus and they were never coerced into changing their belief system.

Kudmul-pijja honestly believed that God could be worshipped in a church, mosque or in a temple as much as in the simple precincts of the Brahmo Samaj.

Probably, his espousal of the principles of the Brahmo Samaj was one of the reasons why he saw the world in the way he did.

Chapter 7
Kudmul-Pijja's Children

Rukmini-amma and Kudmul-pijja's family was a very close one. They had four sons and three daughters. Of the sons, Deva Rao was the eldest. The other three were Amruth Rao, Sanjeev Rao and Madhav Rao.

His second son, Amruth Rao, died of typhoid in 1891, before the development of antibiotics like ciprofloxacin and ceftriaxone.

This affected his father immensely and it took him a year to recover from the loss. Ullal Raghunathaiah helped him get over his depression.

His third son, Madhav, died of an ear infection in Dr Adappa's nursing home in Mangalore.

The last son, Sanjeev Rao, died when he was still in school. The story goes that he was struck by lightning.

Sanjeev Rao and Madhav Rao died before reaching adulthood, as Brahmacharis. They were too young to be married.

The only son who survived, Deva Rao, worked as a clerk in the District Board office. His only son, Sadashiv Rao, was married to Vimala Nagarmath. They lived in the Saraswat colony in Mumbai. They had one son, Jagadish, who died young of burn injuries. After the death of Jagadish at the age of 12, there was no male heir to carry on the family line.

Deva Rao also had two daughters. Sita was married to Balakrishna Moodbidri. They had one son, Uday. The younger daughter, Rukma, married Shankar Mundkur and they have two sons, Sudhir and Gopi.

Kudmul-pijja had three daughters who achieved eminence in their own right: Lalithabai, Radhabai and Shantabai.

Chapter 8

Lalithabai

Lalithabai was the eldest of Kudmul-pijja's daughters. She was probably born in 1886. Her father was born in 1859 so he was twenty-seven when she was born.

As his first daughter, Lalithabai was very close to Kudmul-pijja. She may have come from a relatively poor family, but it was an enlightened and forward-thinking one.

Lalithabai is described as pleasant-looking, though dark, but most of all, very huggable. She was a most likeable person from all reports. Intellectually, Lalithabai was extremely intelligent and articulate. She not only spoke well but also wrote extremely well.

The Harijan movement started by Kudmul-pijja had its repercussions and he was excommunicated. This did not make much of a difference to Kudmul-pijja because by then he had become one of the pioneers of the Brahmo Samaj in Mangalore. When they were excommunicated, his family also became Brahmos; his daughter Lalithabai became and remained a staunch follower until she passed away.

Kudmul-pijja had always believed in the emancipation of women and encouraged his daughters to attend school and college. He sent Lalithabai and Radhabai to a boys' college in Mangalore. They were among the first girls to enter.

However, Lalithabai couldn't complete her Intermediate because Kudmul-pijja got her married to Rao Bahadur N. Subba Rao, the son of Dewan Bahadur N. Shiva Rao, in 1904.

Dewan Bahadur and Diwan Bahadur were titles of honor awarded by the British in India. They were awarded to individuals who had performed faithful service or acts of public welfare to the nation. Dewan literally means Prime Minister in the Indian context and Bahadur means brave. As a matter of fact, Kudmul-pijja was also given the title of Dewan Bahadur, although he never used it.

Dewan Bahadur ranked above Rao Bahadur and people who were titled Rao Bahadur could be elevated to that status. This is what happened to N. Subba Rao, who was initially given the title of Rao Bahadur which was then elevated to Dewan Bahadur.

Dewan Bahadur N. Shiva Rao was a wealthy man; not being rich himself, Kudmul-pijja must have felt his daughter could have a more comfortable life with Subba Rao.

N. Subba Rao was an alumnus of Central College, an institute that was over a century old and was originally was called the University College of Mangalore. It was started as a provincial school in 1868 and was declared a college in 1878.

Subba Rao was a widower. His first wife, whose maiden name was Devi, had been renamed Tara as the custom at the time was that the husband's family gave the bride a new name. Tara died young, leaving behind four children – Paravathibai, Krishna Rao, Radhabai and Rama Rao.

Despite the children and the fact that Subba Rao was a widower with children, Kudmul-pijja arranged Lalithabai's marriage to him. One reason may have been that Subba Rao was also a social worker and had embraced many of the same principles as Kudmul-pijja. The other was that being a wealthy family, they had no expectations from him.

However, in 1904, when Subba Rao married Lalithabai, he married into a family that had been excommunicated. With this single act, he threw in his lot with his father-in-law, joining Kudmul-pijja and showing he was committed to social reform and his father-in-law's ideals.

Of course, Subba Rao was also promptly excommunicated too.

To quote Tara Chandavarkar, Lalithabai's granddaughter, "It was from a family which had been blessed by God but cursed by ignorant men who knew not what the Brotherhood of Man implied that Lalithabai came as a young bride." She entered this wealthy, yet not absolutely orthodox, and English-speaking home of Rao Bahadur N. Subba Rao.

Despite their wealth and standing, in her new surroundings, even though she had the strong backing of her husband, Lalithabai had to face innumerable hardships at the hands of the general public, relatives and domestics. Still, even though she was married young, Lalithabai met this difficult situation with incredible equanimity.

To emphasise the point that they genuinely believed in what they said, Lalithabai and Rao Bahadur N. Subba Rao employed a non-Brahmin domestic help and a Panchnama driver.

All this was totally in violation of old customs and absolutely against the caste system, and there was a good deal of consternation and horror in the community. The Saraswat community was scandalised.

Dewan Bahadur Subba Rao had been left with four motherless children whom Lalithabai had to look after. The love she lavished on these children was returned in equal measure and remained green forever. She never made any difference between her own son and any of the other four children.

In spite of the fact that she had to run a large house, she took time to finish her Intermediate after she became a mother to Shiva Rao.

Lalithabai's husband, Subba Rao, was later appointed to be a District Magistrate in the Madras Presidency before Independence.

Lalithabai and Dewan Bahadur Nyampalli Subba Rao became a well-known couple in Mangalore. Coming from a middle-class Saraswat background, Lalithabai was thrown into a Westernised family. Their ideas and behaviour must have been totally alien to her. However, she became a very good hostess who made her guests comfortable and welcome.

Dewan Subba Rao and his wife, Lalithabai, were prominent citizens of Mangalore; they, to quote *Our Portrait Gallery*, "entertained in his palatial bungalow successive governors – Lord Ampthill, Lord Wenlock, Sir Arthur Lawley, Lord Willingdon and Lord Goschen."

Apart from British visitors, Lalithabai seemed to know the secret of pleasing guests whatever their position in life. *Our Portrait Gallery* again, "Mrs Subba Rao . . . who by reason of her education refinement seemed to know the secret of pleasing guests whatever their rank, wealth, profession of political belief. At different times, Mrs. Gandhi and Sir P. Rajagopalachariar, Dr. Rabindranath Tagore and Mr. F.S. Marvin, Sir. N.G. Chandavarkar, to choose only a few out of a bewildering array of names quite as distinguished, enjoyed the hospitality of his house and were charmed to discover that there was not the slightest discrimination on account of colour, caste, creed or politics. No communal or racial barriers."

Some of these names were engrained on tablets that were embedded on the outside walls of "Shiv Bagh," the ancestral home that, unfortunately, no longer exists.

Lalithabai was elected as a counsellor of the Municipal Council, despite not being highly educated. She was the first-ever lady counsellor and in that capacity tried to help educational institutions as well as institutions that performed social work. Her father's and husband's unflinching support and backing must have been a tremendous help. This was the greatest tribute that the elder men of Mangalore could have paid her. And, the lack of formal education never deterred her from writing beautifully and reading all she could. In fact, reading was Lalithabai's passion and *The Book of Daily Strength* was her constant companion to her last day.

A wonderful illustration of that ability is shown in Lalithabai's letter to Kudmul-pijja when Dewan Bahadur Subha Rao and she were invited to the 1911 Durbar in Delhi.

Madras Provincial Camp

Coronation Durbar

Delhi

5th December 1911

Tent No 14

My Dear Papa,

I feel so cold that my hand does not move freely and hence this writing. I hope when I write a little, I shall be able to write better.

We left Baroda on the 2nd instant at 6:55 pm and arrived here on the 3rd at 7 AM. The journey was not very interesting nor the scenery beautiful. The approach to Delhi was not seen as it was night time.

We are here provided with a tent of two wide rooms each with a veranda 4 feet of all around. There are separate rooms of corrugated iron for kitchen etc. The furniture, stationery etc, are also supplied there (There are eight electric lights used). There are about ten motor cars for the Madras Presidency guests, one for two guests or more. So we drive morning and evening when the ear can be had exclusively at our disposal. Every camp has a complete bazaar from which all materials can be had, good milk, excellent ghee and all kinds of vegetables, all of which not very dear.

If I go on writings about Delhi, I think I can write the whole day. I shall give you all the information when I return, but will write to you occasionally only to give you general news about us. This morning we had been to Kutub Minar about 10 miles from here. There are 374 steps up the pillar. We went to the top and you can imagine how extensive the view around us was. The guide showed us the place formerly called Hastinapura, Prithvi Raja's old fort, now in utter ruins. For miles around are here and there are these ruins of old monuments, buildings, forts and even temples. I have taken a photo of Prithvi Raja's iron pillar with a portion of the Temple behind it and now remaining. I do not know how it will turn out. We then motored to another tomb which has been built in stone in imitation of the Taj.

Why does not any of you write letters to me? Have Shiv Rao and the others gone to Karwar? Delhi is rather cold now especially the mornings and nights. The normal temperature is 41 degrees Fahrenheit. The cold is not pleasant like that of Ooty. It is biting cold and I feel the skin on my legs (she mentions a word in Kannada). I hope you will not show this stupid letter to any of your friends, not even to your friend.

You may tell the purport no 5, 6, storied buildings as in Bombay. But there are light electric tramcars, big buildings etc.

The Durbar camp is simply magnificent. It reflects very great credit to the organisation powers of our government. Each province has its own provincial camp, each governor and his guests at the governors' camp, then there are the chiefs' camps, the king's camp. I cannot describe to you how grand the governors', the chiefs' and the king's camps are. As Delhi is a vast plain all these tents lit up by electricity and some beautifully illuminated with electric lights make the otherwise dry plain a city of tents and I am very poor in words to express in adequate terms, the beauty, the grandeur and the magnificence of this sight at evening time when we motor down. Types of human misery, poverty helplessness are all these to be seen in the town, though full of people but not in the camp. Even the roads, the railway and the stations have been newly made for the Durbar. It appears the place now utilised for tents was used for cultivation. Constructions must have stopped it at least for the last 2 or 3 months. I don't know if this has added or will add to the already prevalent famine.

It is night time and getting very cold I shall stop here.

By the by, I just saw the Princess of Baroda today. She is very fair and beautiful. It is too much to think that at last she will (be) named as a second wife to the Maharaj of Gwalior. Such a priceless gem and looking all goodness in her frank face! You must have read about it in the Indian Social Reforms.

With love,

Yours

Lalitha.

How is (illegible) Please write at least a postcard to us. So glad we have received a letter from you.

Lalithabai and her family respected all religions and thought God could be worshipped in a church, mosque or temple.

Lalithabai and Rao Bahadur N. Subba Rao were married for 30 years. He passed away in Madras in 1934 most likely from complications arising from diabetes. Lalithabai passed away in 1949 in Mangalore in Shiv Bagh, in the same year that Shiva Rao's youngest son, Subban, was born.

Chapter 9
Subba Rao and Lalithabai's Family

Of the family's children, the eldest son, N. Krishna Rao, died of typhoid at the age of 19, leaving behind a child widow, Kamala. She married again and became well known as Kamaladevi Chattopadhyay. She was a freedom fighter in the early years of India, and she refused to become a governor of a state or an ambassador to a foreign country. Instead, through her Indian Cooperative Union, she worked to resettle refugees in North India. From the 1950s, she established the All India Handicrafts Board and headed it for twenty years. According to Ramachandra Guha, "That Indian crafts are still alive and, moreover, have a visible national and international presence is owed more to Kamaladevi Chattopadhyay than to any other individual."

Kamaladevi helped to create other institutions too, including the National School of Drama, the Sangeet Natak Akademi and the India International Centre.

The second son, Rama Rao, married Yamuna Hattikudur. He qualified as a lawyer in India. His father, Subba Rao, wanted him to go and study law in England, but he was adamant that he would not study in the UK while India was still under British rule.

He did not practice law and became a farmer instead, looking after the land around Shiv Bagh and farther away. Rama Rao was the first person to introduce the Japanese method of rice cultivation to South Kanara, which helped the yield per acre increase substantially.

Rama Rao had two daughters, Tara and Shantha.

Tara was married to Narayan Chandavarkar, a brilliant architect who had just started his own company. He died in 1963 at the age of thirty-nine, leaving Tara with four young children to look after. She decided to continue the company with an architect as a partner. She built Chandavarkar & Thakker into a leading architectural firm in South India.

Her sister, Shantha, was married to Arvind Gersappe, who was an engineer qualified from England.

Subba Rao's next daughter, Parvati, was a bit slow. She married Lakshman Rao Balsavar and the couple had three children: Snehlatha, Ganesh and Tara.

Snehlatha married a Tirkanad. The couple had no children.

Ganesh joined the English shipping firm, Calcutta and Burmah Steam Navigation Company in Calcutta. The firm had been formed out of Mackinnon, Mackenzie & Co. He reached a senior position. During the Second World War, he left the box-wallah life and joined the British Indian Army.

Tara was a sweet and gentle soul, loveable and an excellent seamstress. She married Ratnakar Hattikudur. The story goes that they were very much in love. They lived in Sanvordem, Goa and created a furore by going for walks holding hands. The neighbours were outraged and used to look out of their windows to watch this scandalous couple. Tara passed away early leaving behind two children: Indu and Umesh.

Radhabai was the youngest sister and she was married to Raghunathaiah's son, Mangesh Ullal, who became a teacher in Mangalore. They had two daughters, Meera and Sunithi. Meera married Bhaskar Nirody and Sunithi married Prabhakar Kodange. They had three children: Maya, Madan and Mohan.

Subba Rao's last son and Lalithabai's only son, N. Shiva Rao, had asthma and was sent to study in Bangalore at St. Joseph's College. He then studied law at Peterhouse, Cambridge, UK. As a result, he never really got to know Kudmul-pijja very well. Shiva Rao came back in the early 1930s and joined the Imperial Tobacco Company – now known as ITC. He was the first Indian to be invited to join the company's board when he became its Sales Director. Shiva Rao had three children, Praemi, Sheila and Subban.

Praemi, the eldest, was married to Gangolli Manohar Row, the grandson of Vombatkere Pandrang Row, the first Indian Judge of Madras High Court.

Sheila, the second daughter, married Preetam Barua, whose father, Surinder, was in the railways and got to know Shiva Rao when they were both posted in Madurai.

Subban, the youngest, married Sheila Hattikudur, who was the granddaughter of one of Yamuna (né Hattikudur)'s sisters.

Chapter 10

Radhabai

Radhabai, Kudmul-pijja's second daughter, was fair and very striking-looking. She was sent to Madras to complete her graduation. It was there that she met Dr Subbarayan, a non-Brahmin, who was the Zamindar of Kumaramangalam. This marriage was the result of a little romance.

Radhabai was a student of St. Mary's College and had to travel by bus to get there. Dr Subbarayan also used to take the same bus. They saw each other while travelling on the bus every day. They started talking and finally decided they liked each either and wanted to get married.

There was one hitch: he was not a Brahmin, but a Mudaliar. As can be imagined, his family was a bit wary of approaching Kudmul-pijja. But when they went to ask him whether he would give his approval, he did not hesitate for a moment because of his caste. However, unfortunately, Dr Subbarayan was a posthumous child and had no father, which proved to be a bit of a hurdle. So Dr Subbarayan asked C. R. Rajagopalachari to intercede on his behalf. Rajaji persuaded Kudmul-pijja to agree and let the young couple get married.

The marriage was also in line with Kudmul-pijja's views. By allowing his daughter to marry the Zamindar of Kumaramangalam in 1912, he sent another signal of his strong and unequivocal rejection of the caste system.

Kudmul-pijja had only one condition. Dr Subbarayan came from a very rich Zamindar family, while Kudmul-pijja was a poor man with few resources. When Subbarayan's family came to him for his permission, he said yes, but on the condition that Subbarayan's mother agree to welcome his daughter properly. His daughter would have to be treated with respect and dignity and not be ridiculed for her lack of wealth.

Kudmul-pijja organized his daughter Radhabai's marriage with Dr Subbarayan in Madras in 1912, setting an example for inter-caste marriage in the Saraswat community. Chakravarthi Rajagopalacharya was the presiding priest.

Later, when Mahatma Gandhi's son, Devdas Gandhi, wanted to marry Rajaji's daughter, Radhabai went to speak to Rajaji on Devdas's behalf.

Gandhiji was inspired by the simple marriage between Radhabai and Dr Subbarayan, which had been far from extravagant with no dowry or any other gifts. He permitted his son's marriage with Rajaji's daughter. Rajaji organised his daughter's marriage with Devdas Gandhi in a similarly austere manner.

Dr Subbarayan was a freedom fighter. He became a minister in Nehruji's government and died while serving as the Governor of Bombay.

After marriage, Radhabai did her graduation from Presidency College, Madras, becoming one of the earliest Saraswat women to graduate. She was also an elected member of the senate of Madras University.

She also completed her post-graduation from Somerville College, Oxford.

Radhabai became a well-known politician, women's rights activist and social reformer. In 1930, Radhabai, along with Begum Jahanara Shahnawaz, attended the First Round Table

Conference in London to discuss Constitutional reforms, representing Indian women. She also participated in the Second Round Table Conference as well, where she argued unsuccessfully for a five percent reservation for women.

When the Lothian Committee was appointed, Radhabai was a part of it to gauge public opinion over reservations.

Radhabai was elected unopposed to the Rajya Sabha, the Upper House, from a general constituency in 1938 and became its first woman member.

Dr Subbarayan and Radhabai had four children. After the first two children were born, Radhabai and Dr Subbarayan went to England. In fact, the boys were educated at Eton.

The first son, Paramasiva Prabhakar Kumaramangalam, was the 6th Chief of the Army Staff of the Indian Army from 1967 to 1969. He was among the last of the King's Commissioned Indian Officers to be part of the Indian Army and the last KCIO Indian Army Chief.

He had two children: Subarayan, a son, known as Junior, and a daughter, Roshan.

The second son, Gopal, became head of Coal India. He had four children – one son and three daughters.

His first daughter, Gowri, married Ardhanaeaeshwaran. She is known as Gowri Ishwaran and is an educationist and was the founder principal of the Sanskriti School, in New Delhi. The Government of India awarded her the fourth highest civilian honour of the Padma Shri in 2004 for her contributions to the Indian Educational sector.

The third daughter, Rukmani, became an IAS officer, starting her career as a Sub Divisional Officer in Rajasthan; she retired as Additional Chief Secretary. She was married and divorced. She retains her married name, Haldia.

The third child, a son, was named Krishnan and is a businessman. The youngest daughter, Meenakshi, became a special educator and married Ravi Rao; the couple now lives in the US.

Subbarayan and Radhabai's third son, Surendra Mohan Kumaramangalam, went to King's College, Cambridge, serving as President of the Cambridge Union Society in 1938. Kumaramangalam was called to the bar by the Inner Temple. He returned to India in 1939 and participated in the Indian Independence Movement. During his period at Cambridge, he was deeply influenced by Communism, so he later became a communist theorist and a member of the Communist Party of India. He then joined the Indian National Congress and served as Advocate-General for Madras State from 1966 to 1967. He was elected to the Lok Sabha from Pondicherry in 1971 and became the Minister of Steel and Mines from 1971 until his death in 1973 in a plane crash.

Mohan married Kalyani Mukerjee, the niece of the Bengali politician Ajoy Mukherjee in 1943. The couple had a son, Rangarajan Kumaramangalam, and two daughters, Uma and Lalitha. The son was also a minister in the Central government and died quite young. The eldest girl, Uma, married a Bengali and now lives in the Middle East. The youngest, Lalitha, lives in Madras.

Dr Subbarayan's last and only daughter, Parvathi, was born on 15 March 1919. She did her B.A. (Hons.) from the University of Oxford. While in England, she met N.K. Krishnan, who was studying Mathematics at Imperial College, London and they subsequently married.

During Krishnan's stay in the UK, he was actively involved in the nascent struggle for freedom. On his return to India, both Parvathi and he were totally committed to it, resulting in several stints in jail.

N.K. Krishnan and Parvathi joined the Communist Party of India (CPI). Known to the family as 'Gulam,' Parvathi became a CPI stalwart. Husband and wife were both members of Parliament.

N.K. Krishnan had to go underground during the Freedom struggle and the Emergency; family lore says that Parvathi did too.

Parvathi won the Coimbatore Lok Sabha seat in 1957 and 1977 and a by-election in 1974 on a CPI ticket. She was also a Rajya Sabha member in 1954.

Along with her husband, she was at the forefront of strengthening the trade union movement in Coimbatore, especially among textile mill workers and tea plantation workers in Valparai, where she worked extensively during the 1950s.

"The amount of work that Parvathi Krishnan and her husband N K Krishnan put in to organise the mill workers and rally them to (fight) for their rights was immense. She also played a key role in the 1956 wage agreement for mill workers," said M Arumugam, CPI MLA from Valparai.

"Parvathi Krishnan remained steadfast to her political ideology till the end and she was one of the very few prominent women political leaders," said former Madras high court judge K Chandru.

Gulam-akka used to share her rich memories of the historical figures and the lifestyles of contemporary India. She had a daughter, Indira Dasgupta, who is a doctor and now lives in the USA, and a granddaughter, Poornima.

Parvathi Krishnan was 95 years old and was staying alone with two helpers in Coimbatore when she passed away in 2014.

Chapter 11
Shantabai

Kudmul-pijja's third daughter, Shanti, known as Shantabai, was fair and had a wonderful, infectious smile. She was also the most highly qualified of the sisters and became an educationist and academician.

Shantabai helped found the Lady Amritbai Daga College, Nagpur. The college was formally inaugurated by Dr. M.B. Niyogi, the then Vice Chancellor of Nagpur University on the 11th of July 1932 and was affiliated to Nagpur University. It was called the 'Central College for Women' and Shantabai was its first Principal. The famous German architect Otto Konigsberger designed the college – it was the first building he designed in India.

Shantabai later became the head of the Department of Geography at Bedford College in London.

Shantabai never married. After she retired, she came back and lived with her nephew, Shiva Rao, and died in 1970 at their home at Milton Street in Bangalore.

Chapter 12

From Beloved Teacher to Successful Lawyer

Although Kudmul-pijja had worked for some time as a teacher and was well-respected and loved by his students, at some point after 1880, Ullal Raghunathaiah encouraged him to pursue law, believing it would allow him to look after his family better because it would be more remunerative.

So Kudmul-pijja took on the challenge of becoming a pleader, a lawyer who argues in court on behalf of his client. At that time, even a matriculate could sit for the law examination. Apparently, although Kudmul-pijja studied for the examination, he could not appear for it the first time due to his financial circumstances. However, he tried again privately, and this time he completed his pleadership examination.

Kudmul-pijja seemingly seriously considered settling in Bombay Presidency as a pleader of the Bombay High Court because his prospects would have been better with a more financially rewarding future. But when he appeared for the pleader's examination, probably a few years after 1880, he placed in the second class, qualifying him only as a second class pleader in the lower courts of the Madras Presidency.

After he qualified, he resigned from his job as a schoolmaster in the local municipal school. However, his village, Kudmul, and even Mangalore, did not offer very much for bettering one's prospects. Madras was the biggest and nearest city. So Kudmul-pijja moved there and set up practice as a pleader.

After a while, the family is not sure how long, he left Madras and came back to Mangalore to become a pleader in Mangalore District Court.

In the course of the next few years, he earned a name for himself as a successful criminal lawyer. At last, he could earn enough to support his family, which by then consisted of his brother, mother, wife and two sons.

Kudmul-pijja was in great demand among litigants, especially the poor. He would assist the poor, without demanding high fees when he decided they had a just cause. He was often called the 'poor man's lawyer' because of the lengths he would go to help the poor and illiterate to present their cases. Known for his honesty, lack of deceit and transparency in all dealings, he endeared himself to people all around him. People came to him from far and wide with the problems for which they looked towards him to fight their cases.

One story we have all heard is about an upper-class man who raped a Dalit woman and got her pregnant. Normally, at that time, there would have been no compensation for the woman because she was from a lower caste. But Kudmul-pijja argued in favour of the woman and won the case. The Dalit woman received some compensation for her suffering.

As a lawyer, Kudmul-pijja was admired and trusted for his adherence to truth and his strong desire for justice for his clients. He also became the favourite of the district munsiff and the divisional magistrate, especially because he readily went on a circuit to the villages where his cases were posted.

In 1891, his son Krishna Rao died of typhoid fever after an illness of a few days. This gave him a terrible shock and he took a long time to recover. He gave up his law practice for some time and became a recluse.

Ullal Raghunathaiah was a constant companion and good friend to Kudmul-pijja in his time of grief. Raghunathaiah, with great difficulty, persuaded him to go back to work. He encouraged Kudmul-pijja to attend the munsiff court and begin to practice again. Kudmul-pijja finally agreed; however, this time, he took up law on the civil side.

In this practice, Kudmul-pijja rose to eminence within a short time. By 1895 or 1896, he was a leading member of the local Bar in the munsiff court.

THE BIRTH OF A SOCIAL CRUSADER

Chapter 13

The Path to Becoming a Change-Maker

N. Rama Rao told his nieces about an incident Kudmul-pijja's eldest son had narrated. Apparently, Kudmul-pijja had a Roman Catholic client who was a schoolmaster in an elementary school in Kankanady that was run by the Mangalore Municipality. One evening in the course of a conversation on secondary education, the client told Kudmul-pijja that one of the prefects in the school, a Panchnama, Bendur Babu, had passed the primary examination of standard V and was eligible for promotion and to teach the first form. However, he had not been appointed, presumably because of his caste.

Kudmul-pijja did not say anything, staying silent for quite a few minutes. Then, all of a sudden he asked the client to send Bendur Babu to his house the following morning without fail. No one knew his intentions, because Kudmul-pijja never told anybody what he was planning to do. His stated policy was 'Do not talk about what you are going to do, do it.'

The next morning, Bendur Babu came as requested.

Kudmul-pijja questioned Bendur Babu and collected all the information he needed. Then, at some point between 1887 and 1888, when Kudmul-pijja was working as a lawyer in the Mangalore District Court, a British judge began the process to appoint Bendur Babu as a clerk. This is according to Mr Ram Kumar, Taluk Extension Officer of Backward Classes and Minorities.

However, the upper caste lawyers and clerks who worked in the same court were against this appointment and protested. The upper castes even conspired with the judge's wife to have the letter of appointment cancelled.

Probably fearing repercussions because they received many letters, some objecting strongly and some even threatening, the judge's wife did not want this appointment to go through and discouraged her husband. The letters must have frightened her and she was keen that the judge should not get involved in such a contentious issue at such a crucial moment just before his transfer.

The British judge was transferred before he completed the appointment. However, before he left, wanting to appease the upper classes without disappointing Bendur Babu, the judge explained to Kudmul-pijja that he had already issued an appointment letter to Bendur Babu, but it was impossible to protect a Panchnama from the harassment of the upper caste, so Bendur Babu would not be able to lead a peaceful life in Mangalore. Instead, the judge suggested that Kudmul-pijja should find employment for him in a school which admitted children of his caste where he would receive a decent salary.

Kudmul-pijja accepted this proposal because he felt it would be fair to all concerned. But on further thought, he probably realized that Bendur Babu should have got the job because he was qualified. The only reason he did not get it was because of his caste, which was unfair.

It is interesting to contemplate if this incident was one of the many that made him totally change his lifestyle and embrace a life of social service.

But that was definitely not the only reason.

Kudmul-pijja had to travel all over Dakshin Kanara as a pleader. Thus, he was able to see for himself the ugly underbelly of the peaceful and prosperous area in which he lived and now thrived. He saw the degradation and the despair that poverty brings.

He saw first-hand the evils of the caste system. The cruelty meted out to the Dalits and their complete dependence on the good nature of their landlords also made a deep impression on him. He saw how the Panchnamas were relegated to poverty generation after generation and how there was only hopelessness and no expectation for a better life for themselves or for their children.

He saw the condition of jailed prisoners and the condition of young widows. He was an eye witness to the pain suffered by the women especially, child widows and child brides.

These evils would have pained any contemporary thinking person but a man of those times either took this sort of inhumanity for granted or ignored it entirely. So, what is extraordinary is how deeply these experiences affected Kudmul-pijja. Seeing all this made him determined to become the catalyst for change.

He was a man who thought through an issue. So he undoubtedly struggled to reconcile what he had seen with the social conventions under which he had been brought up. We can be sure that Kudmul-pijja agonised about how society, custom and his religion justified, even ratified, the complete separation, the insurmountable wall between the upper and lower castes. But, instead of blindly accepting those strictures, he started to question society's strongly-held beliefs and ideas of the strict differences of caste, creed and sex. How could one human being treat another in ways that were worse than the way they would treat an animal?

Kudmul-pijja was a man of great determination. He became convinced that it was everyone's responsibility to abolish these cruel practices. Everyone, but starting with himself.

He decided that he had to work to remove the practice of untouchability that had ostracized certain castes from society, causing pain, poverty and exploitation. This, even though the caste system had existed in India for hundreds of years. He decided that women had to be treated as equals and widows should not be ostracized. He determined that even criminals were human beings and should not be treated like animals.

All movements are started by one person who believes passionately in the cause. Kudmul-pijja became that one person in this case.

Kudmul-pijja envisioned a society without any differences between one man and another. He saw that this would have to be done not merely through passing laws and enforcing regulations, but by making people see the injustice that was being inflicted on their fellow human beings.

They had to see that the only way forward was to change old ideas and superstitions and regard all as equal.

This aim, although it may seem idealistic, is what led him to give up his practice of Civil Law and take to social service in 1887 when he was just 38.

When Kudmul-pijja made up his mind to give up his lucrative career as a lawyer, he set his aims and objectives for the rest of his life. From what we know, they were mainly the abolition of poverty among Dalits, removal of untouchability from society, empowerment of women, education for all and the rehabilitation of prisoners.

Of course, he helped wherever help was needed.

For example, after the First World War, a great famine hit India. During this period, Kudmul-pijja distributed articles of daily need like rice and kindling wood to the poor in Shedigudde.

In another instance, when the great plague struck Mangalore in 1901, Kudmul-pijja and his son-in-law to-be, N. Subba Rao, picked up dead bodies for disposal, refusing to differentiate between caste, creed, religion and sex.

Chapter 14

Understanding the Horrors of the Caste System

What could have inspired a man like Kudmul-pijja to turn away from a successful career, wealth and a good reputation to follow ideas and aims that went against the rigid social mores, customs and rules of the 1870s? What could have made him brave ex-communication and ostracization from a community where he was highly respected? What could have made him be willing to risk a return to the grinding poverty that characterized his earlier years?

First, it might be worth explaining the situation facing the Panchnamas in the late 19th Century. At the time of Kudmul-pijja, the Dalits were known as Panchnamas or Holeyas in Kannada. Some of the tribal communities were called Adivasis, which translates to original dwellers of the land.

They were all slotted into their level of society by the harsh rules of the Hindu caste system.

The origins of the caste system, although prevalent all over India, has no known historical antecedents. Where the system of exclusion first sprang up is lost in the mists of time. However, it was evidently not there from the beginning because it is believed in South Kanara that the ancestors of the Panchnamas, the Holishekar, ruled as kings. However, this claim is either mythical or, at any rate, not recorded as written history.

Hinduism is known to be a faith that is inclusive and tolerant of others' beliefs. In fact, it has been able to include the gods worshipped by the Panchanamas, like Nanda, the pariah of Chidambaram, and Kanakadasa.

In Udupi, the statue of Kanakadasa still stands in front of the Krishna temple. The myth behind that statue is that listening to his *kirtanas*, Lord Krishna was so pleased that he turned his face towards the East, where Kanakadasa was standing. Today, even though the temple entrance faces the West, the idol of Krishna faces the East.

Even after centuries, the upper caste Hindu admiration for Kanakadasa's piety and devotion has not diminished.

Another story goes that the Indiraja Swami of the Puttige Mutt, knowing the sincerity and earnestness of Kanakadasa, asked each one of his disciples what he held in the palm of his hand. None were able to say what it was except Kanakadasa who affirmed that it was Vasudeva Saligram.

There is a poem in Kannada illustrating that there can be saints from any caste. Any reformer who wants to alleviate their sufferings and uplift them from their degradation has to work against tremendous odds. A spirit of dissatisfaction and discontent has to be aroused in them for them to look for changes and to raise themselves from these present conditions.

However, when it came to the actual treatment of the Panchnamas in their day-to-day lives, the evolved and inclusive tenets of Hinduism were ignored.

As a consequence, the Panchnamas' lives were utterly wretched. The upper castes treated them in a manner that can only be called appalling.

The Panchnamas were considered beyond the pale of Hindu Society by the so-called 'upper caste.' They were slotted even below the class of Sudras in the Hindu caste system and all classes within this lower caste were Untouchables. The Thotis, Mhars, Sudras and Koragas were considered to be almost non-human, the lowest of the low.

So, over a hundred and twenty years ago, what Kudmul-pijja must have seen was that these depressed castes and tribes had to sweat and toil to earn even a morsel of food or a yard of cloth. They were basically hard-working, but the only jobs available to them was to work in fields belonging to rich landlords or in doing jobs no higher caste person would do like cleaning the night soil, removing garbage and sewage.

The conditions of this employment were also heart-rending. These men and women worked their entire lives like animals and with no clothes to cover their bodies. And, for their labour, they received only a specified and limited amount of rice or paddy every day. Further, the Panchnamas were only employed during the season of ploughing and planting the seedlings and during the harvest season, so at other times, they supported themselves by doing any labour-intensive job they could find that the higher castes did not want to do.

The Panchnamas had no houses of their own. In fact, they were not even allowed to own any private property by decree of the caste system. They either lived in dense forests and steep hills or on the edges of the villages and towns of Kanara. In the hills and forests, the Panchnamas survived half-naked. They ate wild animals and birds and edible roots and fruit. For shelter, they built small huts called Koppa, made out of bamboo.

Around the towns and villages, they lived on open grounds in huts built of mud and covered with plaited coconut fronds. Both these huts had only one room where the parents and the children gathered together to eat and to sleep. Their utensils were a few earthenware pots.

Neither of these two kinds of dwellings was comfortable during the heat of the Indian summer. And during the rainy season, the condition of these unfortunates became even more wretched because their hovels could not protect them from the fury of the mighty Indian monsoon.

Their children were mostly unwashed and unkempt and their parents did not even have a thought of sending them to school. In fact, the children were seen as a source of income. They had to help the parents in their work as soon as they could and contribute to family earnings.

It was not exploitation or forced child labour, it was purely for sustenance. The entire family generally lived hand-to-mouth and were always half-starved, with or without the child's income. It was only very rarely that a family could enjoy a full square meal. So, the men, women and children of these communities were malnourished, under-sized and unfit.

In some places, the Panchnamas were serfs. They were attached to the soil, treated like property and sold along with the land. Although, strictly speaking, this sale of human beings was prohibited and completely illegal, the serfs clung to the soil and rarely quit their masters. Even their marriages were performed by their landlords in the northern parts of the district and the landlord was supposed to take care of their children.

Since farming jobs were seasonal and other labour-intensive jobs, although available, did not pay well, they were desperately impoverished. So, the Panchnamas had no choice but to always be dependent on others. In fact, their main source of income was begging.

To make matters worse, although the 'Untouchables' were all styled as Panchnamas by the upper castes, the Panchnamas had divided themselves into many subsets. They identified minute shades of difference that could not easily be discerned by outsiders. They formed their own rigid compartments within their castes where one class was not allowed to mix or associate with another in matters of food and drink, to say nothing of marriage. In a sad mimicry of their own subjugation, the Koragas had developed strata after strata within their own society. And they treated the 'lower' castes with the same contempt and disregard for humanity with which the upper caste Brahmins treated them.

For example, the Mundar Holegas were the highest class among them, the Brahmin class of the Panchnamas so to speak. They did not eat the carcasses of dead animals and did not mix with the other classes whom they consider lower, such as the scavenging class.

So, among them, they had strong prejudices and bigotry that also needed to be overcome.

The Panchnamas had no individual freedom nor were they aware of the concept of human rights. And to the upper caste people, the laws of the land did not apply to the Panchnamas or Koragas.

For example, if a lower caste man dared to fall in love with a Brahmin lady, he would be put to death. However, if a Brahmin fell in love with a lower caste lady, all he had to was to undergo a *Payachit* or purification ceremony. Likewise, if a higher class man killed a lower caste person, there was no punishment but a lower caste man who killed an upper caste person was instantly put to death.

The belief was that if a Koraga's shadow fell on a Brahmin, the Brahmin would have to purify himself by doing the

Prayashchitam or risk a disaster in his next life. So the Panchnamas were made to stand yards away, or even move across the road when a Brahmin passed by.

They were prohibited from drawing water from wells owned by the upper caste for fear of contamination, so they had to use public wells, ponds and rivers.

This vile treatment of Panchnamas happened as a matter of course, even in enlightened families.

Recently, Kudmul-pijja's granddaughter, Praemi, and some of her friends were reminiscing about their childhood days in Mangalore. One of them remembered incidents that highlight the indignity and the cruelty of treating others as Untouchables.

At the time of Diwali, all the domestic help were given clothes for the year, from the Brahmin cook to the sweeper ladies. But these unfortunate Thotis were not allowed to come anywhere near the house. Instead, they had to stand a distance away and the ladies of the house would throw the clothes to them. It didn't matter if the clothes fell to the ground. This way, by the standards of the caste system, neither the house nor the lady was polluted.

It wasn't just about clothes.

After all these years, older members of the family still have memories of the Thoti men and women coming every day to clear away the night soil. The latrines were always a short distance from the main house, so these people were always invisible to the upper caste family members.

Looking back, Praemi and her friends didn't know whether to laugh or cry because they used to think this was completely normal. In fact, many members of the family wonder how the cruelty and inhumanity of these practices did not strike them. It just did not occur to them that these 'scavengers' were not being given any respect or shown any kindness. They were not just untouchable, they were unknowable and unrecognizable.

The Panchnama classes behaved in ways that were probably brought about by shabby treatment and centuries of servitude. They had their own caste meetings where the word of the elders or the *Gurikar* was law. The Gurikar were treated as the head of the community and the caste members followed their orders unquestioningly. These orders superseded any injunction laid down by national legislation or the upper castes. Dereliction of conduct in caste matters invited severe punishment, so no caste member dared to disobey the commands of the Gurikar.

Further, there were a number of social customs that the members of the caste had to observe. Those in breach of these unwritten rules were tried and their punishment was decided at meetings held for the purpose where the punishment was meted out.

The Panchnamas believed in witchcraft and worshipped gods and goddesses who were conceptualized as 'evil' spirits or *'Bhootas'* like Panjul, Karunanthaya and Guniliga. There were yards in front of the villages dedicated to their worship, where shrines were constructed that contained wooden images that were decorated in times of 'Bhootakate' or annual festivals like Nemedud and Kalu. These gods were all spirits in whose honour animal sacrifices had to be made to propitiate them and dissuade them from evil.

The Panchnamas had songs in local languages that relate anecdotes that described the exploits of these Bhootas. The story-songs tell of the prowess and power of these spirits.

During the *Bhootakate*, the gods or goddesses were said to enter the body of a dancer, sending him into a trance. While in that state, he would bless members of the audience.

All this was followed with great attention by onlookers and they considered themselves highly fortunate if they were blessed.

Often these Bhootakate ended in disputes leading to fights among the rival factions. The likelihood of this happening was further aggravated by free-flowing liquor. These fights often resulted in bloodshed and grievous injuries.

Bhootakate was a common and well-established practice in the district and among the Dalits. For most upper castes, it was a disturbing and frightening experience to attend and watch the events at these Bhootakates.

Of course, on occasion, the festivals were orderly and members were well behaved. However, these occasions were few and far between.

Kudmul-pijja staunchly opposed the Bhootakate because he felt what happened at the event was anti-social. He used to try and explain to the Panchnamas the futility of this celebration because it almost always ended in violence, bloodshed and grief. He would hold evening meetings where he would explain the value of integrity and unity among themselves.

Although the Panchnamas gathered in large numbers and listened patiently, he was not always successful in convincing them to give up these practices. After centuries of adhering to them, they did not recognise the need for change or the difference it would make to their lives.

Kudmul-pijja also discouraged begging because he believed it was an affront to human dignity. However, the upper castes, including the Saraswat community, were scared that with education and empowerment, the Panchanamas would rise and claim equality, which meant they would no longer be willing to be bonded labour – almost slaves. So Kudmul-pijja knew very well from the very start that it was not going to be easy to accomplish their empowerment.

One example of the work he did was his attempts to rehabilitate the Koraga tribe.

The circumstances under which the Koraga tribe lived in those days was unimaginably wretched. The Koraga were abysmally poor and nomadic. They owned no land and were ridiculed and, even worse, were chased away if they entered the town in search of even the most poorly-paid jobs. Kudmul-pijja had a soft corner for them because of their poverty and lack of any kind of hope and he was determined to do something about their plight.

His first attempt was when the Koraga community was, as usual, playing their drums and flutes while disguised as women and dancing in front of shops trying to get alms.

Kudmul-pijja brought them to his school and patiently explained why this was not a good practice. He spoke to them as one would address children, telling them, "Begging makes you a parasite and a drain on society."

But to get the Koragas to change their ways was almost impossible without self-motivation. They were a childlike and innocent people and their only means of survival was to be cunning and sly.

While distributing money to the youth of these tribes, Kudmul-pijja told them to accept the money as a gift and not as alms, but to use it as a step to achieving their dreams. He was keen that they find ways and means to give up these practices. He made them take an oath that they would give up begging and depending on others bounty.

But a few days after this incident, he found they had forgotten about their promise to him and started their usual practice of begging in disguise once again.

Some years later, in 1923, Kudmul-pijja established the Court Hill Adi Dravida Cooperative Society in Shedigudde with the aim of achieving the economic development of the Panchnamas. He believed cooperation was one way to help lift them from the quagmire of poverty.

Kudmul-pijja had multiple difficulties in handling the problems of the Panchnamas classes, but to him, it was unthinkable and unbearable that the 'born right' ones could treat people who were 'born wrong' so badly. With this belief, total commitment and unbounded enthusiasm, he drew the attention of the public to the unfairness of the system and initiated several actions to help them.

Chapter 15
Attacked for His Beliefs

Today, it is practically impossible to understand and appreciate the odds Kudmul-pijja would have had to face to help the Panchnamas to break the chains of caste and learn how to respect themselves. Or to understand the difficulty of espousing the belief that this would in turn automatically earn them the respect of the upper classes.

To even begin to understand, we must remember that Kudmul-pijja started his mission a good forty years before Ambedkar and Gandhi. Dr Ambedkar was only born in 1891 in Mhow, by which time Kudmul-pijja had already crystallized his ideas and begun his work.

It is hard to imagine that he began his crusade in the 19th Century. Even today, so many years later, although the tide is turning and thinking is changing, we still hear of the lynching of Dalits for daring to challenge the dictates of caste. We still see news reports of the conflict between the so-called lower and upper castes. We still see how an Adivasi boy can be lynched for riding a white horse to his wedding.

It was only after Independence that the government really realised and addressed the problems of the Scheduled Castes and Scheduled Tribes (SCs and STs). Dr Ambedkar was one of the guiding spirits who had personal experience of the disparities in society and made reservations for them mandatory after Independence.

But, at the time that Kudmul-pijja began his crusade, it was a physically dangerous and socially condemned task to work for the upliftment of the socially downtrodden. It required the courage and commitment of men like Kudmul Ranga Rao to show us the cruelty of the system and the need for change.

Understandably, the uneducated and downtrodden Panchnamas were not able to even comprehend the need to initiate social change or to embrace new ideas and a new way of living either. The Panchnamas were scared of the upper castes and had grown accustomed to their way of life. They believed in fate and did not see how their pre-ordained path could be changed.

It was a difficult job for Kudmul-pijja to make them understand the need for education and skill development and to help eradicate untouchability.

The majority of upper-caste Hindus were not supporters of his ideas at all. They feared that if the depressed classes were educated and became economically stable, then there would no bonded or cheap labourers to work for them. They would also have nobody to do the jobs no upper caste person would do, like cleaning the night soil. As a result, the upper caste constantly pressurized the depressed class not to co-operate with Kudmul-pijja.

This also made the Panchnamas even more hesitant and fearful.

Kudmul-pijja and his family encountered a dismissive attitude from his friends and relatives in addition to the lack of cooperation from the people he was trying to help.

Of course, some members of the upper caste did help, but the majority were actively against him. In fact, the members of the forward caste were often actively and openly hostile to him and his family. His family and he had to face abuse, humiliation and torture from the upper caste.

There were times when night soil was thrown on the balconies of his home. The family faced threats of physical violence from the more traditional members of the community. People not only sneered at Kudmul-pijja's daughters when they were on their way to their schools and colleges, but the girls even had stones thrown at them. Scandalously and outrageously to the conservative people of the time, the girls dared to cycle to college. They did this in the face of jeers from the rowdy elements among the public who disapproved of their father's activities. Of course, although Kudmul-pijja allowed the girls to ride a lady's bicycle to college, he insisted that they should wear blouses with high necks and long sleeves up to the wrists. (Ahead of his times though he undoubtedly was, evidently he had certain limits!)

Kudmul-pijja had to handle other humiliations.

Barbers refused to shave him, dhobis refused to wash his clothes, and domestic help was not easy to get. Even boatmen refused to carry him on their boats to cross the rivers.

In rain or shine, people in South Kanara still carry an umbrella called *Tengane Halle* made from the *kendi* leaf, a certain type of a leaf available locally. Kudmul-pijja was mocked and ridiculed when he carried it. People called out, *"Kerenge Rayar bartherai,"* which, in Tulu, means a foreigner is coming.

But Kudmul-pijja carried on with his mission fearlessly.

Initially, Kudmul-pijja fought for his causes while simultaneously working as a lawyer in the civil court. In fact, his greatest achievements as a successful lawyer happened when the

Head of the Judiciary happened to be the strongest opponent of his religious and social reform ideas.

The attack that came then must have been the hardest to take, because he was a man who believed in prayer and the Almighty.

It so happened that Ullal Raghunathaiah had refused to use Brahmanical rites as prescribed by the Saraswat community while performing his mother's obsequies after her death in 1891. Despite knowing, or maybe knowing that this would have its consequences, Kudmul-pijja had joined Raghunathaiah and helped him to perform the obsequies under Vedic rites and had also partaken of the after-funeral meal.

It was also at this time that Mathadipathy of the Saraswat community visited the court on his tri-annual tour. Sujir Raghunathaya, then District Munsiff of Mangalore and a leading member of the Saraswat community, was deputed by Shri Pandurangashram, the then Anand Ashram Swamiji of the Saraswats, to make an enquiry into the matter and then report back to him.

Kudmul-pijja and Raghunathaiah were questioned concerning their conduct in this matter.

The brothers-in-law were placed in a difficult position. They were both members of the bar who practised before the district munsiff and depended on the goodwill of the judicial head for a successful practice. But nevertheless, both of them had the courage and the conviction to answer the munsiff's questions honestly. They both professed and openly justified their opposition to the social and religious customs they did not believe in.

Shri Pandurangashram Swamy was the eighth *sant* (saint) or Guruji of the Saraswat community and by that time had reigned for over forty years. He was ordained into *Sanyasa,* at the age of twelve. Sanyasa is a form of asceticism marked by the renunciation of material desires and prejudices, represented by a state of disinterest and detachment from material life. The purpose of Sanyasa is to ensure that those who undertake it live a peaceful, love-inspired, simple spiritual life. Shri Pandurangashram Swamy was trained under the earlier Guruji for five years.

He did much good in his time. He ensured that the greater part of the Math was rebuilt and all the samadhis of his predecessors were reconstructed with silver. In the village of Shirali, he built a school, a post office and other institutions that were required by the people. He was a scholar of Vedic astrology and The Vedas.

Still, although he was evidently a man of great learning and made huge contributions to the community, he was set in his ways and rigid in matters of caste. So, after hearing the results of the enquiry, Shri Pandurangashram Swamy declared that both Kudmul-pijja and Raghunathaiah would be suspended from the caste and they were to be banned from entering the temple. As a result, most other members of the Saraswat community ostracised them.

Their ex-communication must have seemed final and irrevocable. However, ex-communication in the Saraswat community was never really permanent.

Shri Pandurangashram attained Mahāsamādhi in 1915. Mahāsamādhi, the great and final samādhi (Perfect union of the individualized soul with infinite spirit), is the act of consciously and intentionally leaving one's body at the moment of death. In Hindu or Yogic traditions, that means that a realized master has consciously left their body, often while in a deep, conscious meditative state.

So, in 1915, the *peetha* (seat) was then ascended by Shri Anandashram Swamiji. He was ordained hardly eight days prior to the Mahāsamādhi of Shri Pandurangashram Swamiji, so he was not guided or influenced by him. He improved the financial position of the Math, which had dwindled during his early years, by making payments of *Vantiga* almost mandatory. He reigned for 51 years and travelled widely. He was widely held to be a virtuous man and saintly in his approach.

Shri Anandashram Swamiji reviewed the case and decided that Kudmul-pijja and Raghunathaiah could be readmitted to caste and religious ceremonies and functions if they offered certain prayers and paid some fines.

Kudmul-pijja was a strong believer in the Almighty. So, after paying the penalties, Kudmul-pijja was taken back into the community.

Kudmul-pijja was apparently 'Gandhian' in his ways and means of persuasion long before Gandhiji. He handled the animosity, mockery, ostracization, ex-communication and even physical abuse with patience, intelligence and a smile. He did not show any signs of frustration or anger. And he did not retaliate in kind, nor did he allow his Panchnama students to reply with violence to these abuses. He persuaded people to abandon age-old customs and practices with humour, gentleness and great patience. He never resorted to violence and kept his temper in check.

He also understood that it would be fruitless to appeal to the sentiments of the upper caste. There was no logic or emotional appeal that could persuade them to work for the cause of reforming the society. The only way forward was to change their mindset.

Going by Yajnavalkya's words to Janaka, Kudmul-pijja possessed *atma*, the mind that does not fear death or yearn for life. The mind that does not seek validation from the outside world. The mind that witnesses the world as it is.

Kudmul-pijja saw his way as the *Dharma Marg* or Right Path, which he knew would give all a better future. It was the right and peaceful path shown by the men through the ages like Buddha, Basaveshwara, Swami Vivekananda and Swami Dayananda Saraswati. He became absolutely determined to work for this great cause, in the process sacrificing his and his family's social standing.

Despite all the obstacles that faced him, Kudmul-pijja made every effort to instil in the socially and economically backward classes a sense of social and intellectual awareness.

As his granddaughter Tara Chandavarkar once said, "In his household and family, there was an atmosphere which taught that one's vision should not be limited to the narrow boundaries of one's own family but should extend to include all those whom help could possibly be given."

In fact, all of them, N. Subha Rao, Lalithabai and Kudmul-pijja, were not mere dreamy-eyed idealists who just spoke on what should be. They were hard-headed and practical doers who set out to achieve their aims at tremendous costs to their personal lives and their standing in society.

Pondering over what then must have seemed an insurmountable task, Kudmul-pijja must have often gone back to one of his favourite maxims. It was one that his daughters often quoted.

"I shall pass thru' this world but once; any good thing that I can do

Or any kindness that I can show to any human being

Let me do it now.

Let me not defer it or neglect it.

For I shall not pass this way again."

– William Arthur Ward

When Kudmul-pijja's grandchildren were young and complained that they were tired and could not do something because it was too difficult, their grandmother would read a poem to them about a small earnest engine that used to pull a train behind him:

"One day he was chugging along the tracks when he saw a small hill in front of him. He looked at it and said, 'I can't pull those carriages up that hill. I know I can't, I know I can't.'

He looked around him but there was no one else to help him so he knew that he had to do it himself. But, he was not going to give up so easily, he pulled the wagons up the hill, saying, 'I know I can. I know I can.'

In no time at all, he was on the top of the hill. And then he gleefully shouted, 'I knew I could! I knew I could!'"

When he was faced with such daunting tasks that involved changing the society's practices and opening people's minds to new ideas, Kudmul-pijja may have repeated to himself the little motto that the children's grandmother recited, "I know I can. I know I can."

Chapter 16

"A Tree Must Be Judged by Its Fruit." Lalithabai's Memorial Speech

Ranga Rao, the subject of this sketch, was a child of poverty. He was brought up in the environment of need and deprivation. With most of us, when one has so little, it is difficult to make life sustainable; it crushes the spirit in us. It makes us very self-centred, mean and selfish, envious of the 'haves.'

The 'have-nots' then become the slaves of the wealthy, dependent on the mercy of the rich and affluent. It destroys people's individuality and self-respect. Humility changes to grovelling at the feet of the rich. Poverty is dreaded by most because it kills our liberty of thought and action. It wipes out qualities which makes us human – it makes us playthings of others. We do not just become the toys of the more powerful, but we easily get into the company of the evil-minded and the wicked. Poverty makes one give in to all sorts of vices that we hope will make life more comfortable. This is coupled with criminal offences affecting both body and mind.

Extreme deprivation, poverty and lack of any basic necessities become a serious problem to solve for political leaders and statesmen. They need to remove poverty and the stigma from the people who suffer from it. All the ways and means at the disposal of the rich and powerful have to be adopted, whereby extreme distress may be removed. Many organisations and institutions need to be formed to remedy this evil and the political machinery must get involved to alleviate the suffering and deprivations of the masses from poverty.

Even today, a hundred and fifty years after Kudmul Ranga Rao lived, we still have deep and pervasive poverty across India. A large number in India still go to bed hungry, malnutrition among children is still common and all the schemes and plans that the Government of India has formulated to provide shelter to all our citizens have not been completely successful.

India is lucky that men like Kudmul Ranga Rao worked to remove this imbalance. It is not difficult to imagine why he felt the need to do his little bit to help those who needed help and what made him choose his life's aims. To be rich and powerful is in a way to be completely cut off from the poverty and the hopelessness which is around us.

Kudmul Ranga Rao was not a rich man, but poverty never had a debasing effect on him because he was never particularly attracted to wealth. Royalty who ruled large empires were no exceptions, and abdicated their thrones in favour of their descendants and took to the life of hermits. In Hindu scriptures these four attributes are expected to be followed as paths to spiritual advancement and growth: they are *Dharma*, *Artha*, *Kama* and *Moksha*.

Hinduism like all the other religions encourages charity – making lives better for the others, feeding the hungry, giving arms and building places of worship. *The Gita* says it is a sin to take without giving back to society.

It is a thief who takes and returns not.

Bhachirhari in his classical poem *vairagya strotam sloka* (doubt) 45 thus describes the pleasure in poverty.

"Look, now the beggar there free from the thraldom of all desires is lying quite like a king, the earth his magnificent bedstead, his arms his pillows, the sky his canopy, the moon his lamp and self-renunciation his lifemate in whose company he enjoys his felicity while four quarters of the globe fan him like true wives."

Wealth produces its own evil effects: it can create an attitude of insecurity with the fear of losing all one has acquired, again, wanting more and more of wealth and fame willing to sacrifice all for the sake of more possessions makes one not always happier. It requires self-control and to say no to overcome desires. This is doubly difficult when the world worships money and fame, power and honour to give it all up. It is regarded as one of the impediments to one's spiritual growth. It requires strength of mind and conviction to overcome the desire of wealth.

Chapter 17
Other Social Activists

Kudmul-pijja was not the only person to dream of a better future. There were many men who were impacted by the injustice of the evils of the caste system, the fact that women were treated like chattels, the illiteracy among the poor and how certain castes were treated worse than animals.

Men like Karnad Sadashiva Rao and Sri Gopalaswamy Iyer, who were contemporaries of Kudmul-pijja, were also social activists with similar ideas. At one time, two of them stayed in South Kanara for two months trying to persuade the people of the upper caste to alleviate the state of the Untouchables and deal with their desperation and their hunger to better their lives.

They were successful in convincing a few of them. But in general, they faced hostility and an absolute and profound rejection of these ideas.

Karnad Sadashiva Rao also helped Kudmul-pijja to start primary schools for Panchnamas, but before the project had progressed very far, he heard a speech given by Gandhiji and joined the Congress Party. It was unfortunate in one way because when Karnad Sadashiva Rao joined the Freedom Movement, Kudmul-pijja lost a valiant worker and companion. Of course, the Freedom Movement gained a stalwart supporter.

Sadashiva Rao probably would have done much more to help the lower castes had he not met Gandhiji and joined the Freedom Movement. However, he was the one responsible for bringing the Annual Congress Samelan to Palace Grounds,

Bangalore. Now the up-market residential area Sadashivnagar in Bangalore is named after him.

This has been remembered and confirmed by Sadashiva Rao's daughters Radhakka and Sagunakka in *Apostles of Peace*.

In a small coincidence, Kudmul-pijja and Karnad Sadashiva Rao are partners again because the roads named after them in Mangalore join each other.

Chapter 18

An Absolute Commitment to Education

During the middle of the 19th century, South Kanara was part of the Madras Presidency, ruled by the British. The British were keen to see the development and the upliftment of the lower castes and the administration of the time had set up a separate department for the welfare of the socially depressed classes. Certain programmes like the establishment of colonies, wells, distribution of government lands and so on were undertaken. They also instituted separate schools.

One such school was at Valencia in Mangalore (near the north side of Welfare School, near Father Mueller's Hostel, Kankanady). This school provided free mid-day meals for the students.

At about the same time, Kudmul-pijja had refined his vision for the Panchnamas. His dream was to create a new generous society where the deprived would be empowered with equal opportunities to make them better citizens, educated and employable.

To achieve these ambitions, he decided that the only way forward was for the Panchnamas to be educated and to acquire skills that would give them financial security. He imagined a solution that resonates today and is still valid, viable and much needed.

As a former teacher, he had the foresight and wisdom to see that the education of all men and women, of whatever caste, creed or religion, was the only way the have-nots could be shown hope.

Only education could help them to achieve all they had so far just dreamt of.

Only education could instil in them the confidence that success was not a dream but they could make a better life.

Only education could banish the horrors inflicted by the caste system and the consequent poverty.

However, as he well knew, the children from the various Dalit communities were not welcome; in fact, they were not allowed to enter any educational institution. He believed that was the reason why they grew up economically, socially and physically underprivileged.

So, in 1892, with his own funds, Kudmul-pijja started his first school in a property rented from a Catholic gentleman. Urva Chilimbi was 50 miles from Mangalore and started as a primary school in a thatched house.

However, education for the Dalits was anathema for the upper caste. They were scared that if the Dalits became educated and economically independent, they could no longer be manipulated and – God forbid – they might actually become aware of their capabilities beyond what their caste dictated they could and could not do. So, although only a few Panchnama children attended the school, the upper castes were furious.

So furious, that a group of the upper caste people made common cause with anti-social elements. They collected the filth which was discarded by the city municipality near Petlandpet and poured it at the entrance of the school. To make things more difficult, they used stones to obstruct entry to the school.

Though Kudmul-pijja complained to the owner, nothing could be done. In the end, he was forced to close the school.

Though the school at Chilimbi was closed, Kudmul-pijja did not lose heart. He had the willpower to carry on his mission to educate the socially depressed with no exceptions.

Kudmul-pijja spoke to the Panchnamas and found out where this kind of school could be better founded; using this information, he started his school for boys in January in 1895 in a small abandoned building in Bolur. The school was intended to give an education to some eight or ten boys, starting with the rudiments of knowledge in the form of reading, writing and arithmetic.

Kudmul-pijja had tremendous odds to overcome to establish this institution, mainly on three accounts: the school, understandably for those days, found it difficult to find a qualified teacher because teachers were generally from a higher caste. Secondly, it was with great difficulty that Panchnama children could be tempted to attend the school. Finally, the parents too had to be made aware of what education could do for their children.

To battle the perception that by sending the children to school the family would be deprived of an earning member, Kudmul-pijja paid one or two annas to the parents as an incentive for them to allow their children to attend school. This was to make up for the money the children would have earned by working.

But boys would still not come to school, notwithstanding the incentives Kudmul-pijja offered. Lower caste parents still preferred that their boys work so that the money they earned could be used for their daily needs.

Further, in an additional expense, slates, books and food had to be provided for the boys. As a result, classes were held very irregularly.

The opposition from the upper caste Brahmins living around the Bolur school also continued unabated. Upper caste men who opposed to his work threw night soil on the veranda of the school. Boys attending the school were beaten up. Even a teacher of the school who was passing by wearing a shirt and carrying a cloth umbrella was roughed up.

This school too was closed down after some time.

But Kudmul-pijja was not daunted by the success or the failure of the schools. He kept persevering in his efforts to give the Panchnama children the benefit of an education and foster the realisation among the Panchnama elders about the knowledge of the advantages of educating the children.

Kudmul-pijja was mockingly called the Guru of the Panchnamas and his wife was called Panchnamati by people passing them on the roads.

However, in spite of the opposition, the next school continued to grow slowly. After some years, the school was found to be too small and a new building had to be constructed. A site was secured from the government below the Court Hill and the expenses for the buildings came from government grants and donations. Kudmul-pijja obtained more money from whatever private resources he had and they contributed towards the cost of the construction.

It is interesting to know that poor as he was, Kudmul-pijja had insured his life for Rs. 2000 and he borrowed money against that for this project.

Kudmul-pijja also realised that to help the Panchnamas climb the social ladder, certain programmes would have to be adopted. He tried to persuade his friends and colleagues to actively participate in implementing these programmes.

After much effort, classes were opened and the arduous task of generating the enthusiasm for the idea of education continued. He also needed to create an enthusiasm in friends and well-wishers for their cooperation and help.

Since it was a school for the Untouchables and teachers were very hard to find, they had to be really well compensated for taking up these jobs. To give the students skill development, they had to find devices as a means of their becoming financially independent. Some skills like carpentry and weaving, tailoring and then silkworm cultivation were started, hoping this would furnish sufficient attraction for the Panchnama children to be drawn towards it. These skills also served to capitalize on the cultural heritage they already had.

His vision was to raise the Panchnamas out of the morass of poverty and discrimination they had suffered for years. First and foremost of the realisation of these dreams was to start primary schools all over the district. He was not deterred by the resistance he faced and the financial difficulties; over the years, he finally succeeded in opening and running a small chain of Panchnama schools. By the time he gave up his work and took Sanyasa, Kudmul-pijja had set up or helped to set up schools in Attavar, Doddakadur, Ullala, Talapadi, Thokkorsu, Moolky and Udupi to name just a few.

However, Kudmul-pijja found it an uphill task to run and manage the schools he had established in far-flung places on his own, even with the encouragement and help from friends and well-wishers. So, in 1897, Kudmul-pijja and Ullal Raghunathaiah established the Depressed Class Mission or DCM in Kodialbail in Mangalore on land leased in Kapikadu from Nellikays Venkata Raju. Ullal Raghunathaiah was the President and Kudmul-pijja the secretary of the Depressed Class Mission.

The stated aim of the institution was the upliftment of the Dalits. The means chosen to achieve this aim was to spread education for one and all, to teach skills to make the underprivileged employable and to provide a religious foundation. All the reforms Kudmul-pijja and Raghunathaiah had initiated were now under the auspices of DCM.

The establishment of the DCM and the school at a time when the upper caste considered themselves so superior that even the shadow of an untouchable falling on them was considered inauspicious was an amazing achievement.

DCM provided support and shelter from ridicule and derision from upper-class children and their parents. DCM and its sister institutions – like the hostels, refuge homes and industrial training units for skill development – became well known in the district for the work they were doing.

But DCM was far from being just a school. It was a potent weapon in the hands of Kudmul-pijja and Ullal Raghunathaiah.

Chapter 19

How Kudmul-Pijja Ran the DCM School

When it came to running the DCM school, Kudmul-pijja was a strict disciplinarian. In the DCM school, education apart, cleanliness and neatness were stressed upon. The children were given two pairs of hand-woven shirts every year. These had to be washed every day and were never allowed to get dirty.

He made it compulsory for the children to wear only *swadeshi* (domestically produced) clothes. This was at a time when there was a slow awakening that there was an exploitation of Indian goods like hand-woven cloth which was replaced by material woven in Manchester UK and sold in India. This threw many local weavers out of employment, causing misery and increasing poverty. Hence, Kudmul-pijja instituted the rule that made it compulsory for his students to wear material made in India. He was adamant that this rule be followed.

Kudmul-pijja himself dressed simply. The clothes he wore were *panche* or *Veshti* (a long unstitched cloth tied at the waist and extending to the ankles), a swadeshi shirt and a towel tied around his head to keep away the heat of the sun.

Kudmul-pijja was a believer in the Divine and this devotion was what he wanted the children to imbibe. In the mornings, the children were woken up at 5.30 and taught prayers, which they chanted in unison. After prayers, the children studied until 8.30. When studies got over, they had breakfast and then they had to run to school.

Every evening, after their studies, the children had to have a bath, change into clean clothes and sit down again for their prayers.

Despite his ex-communication and ostracization, Kudmul-pijja ensured that every day, the children chanted devotional songs to God both in the mornings and evenings. This practice has carried on till the present day.

At DCM, the children were taught and they learnt prayers of all religions so as to understand and imbibe the principle of unity among all. Some of the prayers that were taught to them and they recited worshipfully included:

Gayatri Mantra:

Aum Bhoorbhuvah Svah

Tat savitur varenyam

Bhargo devasya dheemahi

dhiyo ye nah pracho dayet

(Oh creator of the universe we meditate upon the supreme splendour May they radiant power illuminate our intellect destroy our sins and guide us in the right direction.)

Shri Gopal Hattiangadi

Guru Stotram-

Tvameva mata pitaa tvameva

Tvameva bandhu sakhaah tvameva

Tavameva vidhyaa dravinam tvameva

Tvameva sarvam mama deva deva

(You alone are my mother, father, brother and companion. You alone are knowledge and prosperity. O Lord, you mean everything to me.)

Verse from the *Holy Quran*:

Have you observed him who belies religion?

That is he who repels the orphan,

And urges not the feeding of the needy.

Ah, woe up to worshippers

Who are heedless of their prayer,

Who are seen (at worship),

Yet refuse small kindnesses!

Among Kudmul-pijja's papers was a beautiful Christian hymn. It is very likely that the children were taught this knowing Kudmul-pijja's respect for all religions. It happens to have been one of Mahatma Gandhi's favourite hymns as well.

Abide with me.

Abide with me; Fast falls the even tide:

The darkness deepens; lord, with me abide

When other helpers fade, and comforts flee

Help of the helpless, O abide with me

I need thy presence every passing hour;

What but thy grace foil the tempter's power?

Who like thy self my guide and stay can be?

Through cloud and sunshine, O abide with me

In the evenings, in their leisure time, the children were encouraged to play games like tennis, badminton and chess. They could even garden if they wished – in fact, the children had the freedom to do whatever they wanted for recreation.

Health checks were a regular feature of the academic year. Kudmul-pijja believed in cleanliness and good health for the children. Before their evening meal, the children had to wash up and there was time kept aside for prayers.

The schools and their students observed all the festivals throughout the year. They were made to bathe once a day and as a result, they looked clean and healthy.

Gurukulas of yore must have followed the same way of life for the student community.

There was another interesting initiative that Kudmul-pijja undertook to help the Panchanmas integrate into society. These communities almost always named the children after the environment they lived in or animals such as crabs and crocodiles. Perhaps this was done to make these children and adults more identifiable with the distinctly different names.

However, it also clearly identified them as lower caste.

So Kudmul-pijja's next plan was to change the way the Panchnama boys and girls were named. He persuaded the parents to give them names like the higher classes did, after Hindu gods and goddesses and rivers and flowers. In this, he was more successful.

The flag of the DCM school was unusual but relevant to its cause. The school had designed it in its own unique way that conveyed the aims and aspirations of the organisation. The flag showed a Muslim, a Hindu and a Christian sitting on a platform or step of a tall edifice on which stood a lady. In one hand she carried the Union Jack, the national flag of the United Kingdom; the other was stretched out to help the Untouchables pull themselves out of the bog of poverty.

Besides the slogan, the top of the flag depicted the motto of the school: *Deenoddharanam,* upliftment of the depressed classes, and *Deshoddharanam, the* welfare of the state. The flag was carried by the children on all important national days.

The DCM school was a well-thought-out and planned initiative to impart an education combined with discipline and physical activity. It was admired by people of the area.

Most importantly, it achieved Kudmul-pijja's aim, which was to make it difficult for strangers to distinguish a Panchnama boy from those of any other community or caste.

Sri Govinda Rao of Udupi – a freedom fighter who later participated in Gandhiji's eradication of untouchability movement – served as a teacher for 18 years and also as the headmaster of DCM.

The DCM school was exemplary. In fact, the quality of education imparted there was so high that over a period of time, even upper-caste parents used to send their children there.

In a crowning achievement, in 1922, students from the depressed classes were admitted to the High School of the Government College. Some of the most well-known students were Sri B Chandrasekhar, Sri Ramakrishna Udupi and Sri Udyavara Ramachandra.

The success of the DCM school meant that Kudmul-pijja could also start and keep running a chain of elementary Panchnama schools in places in Mangalore, Udupi, Nejaru, Ullal, Mulki and Bannanje in Udupi. He also set up or helped to start schools in Attavar, Doddakadur, Ullala, Talapadi, Thokkorsu, Moolky and Udupi to name a few.

In these schools, the students could study up to the fourth standard; then they were encouraged to do their teacher's training so as to be able to work as teachers in the school they had studied in. In some cases, former students even opened new schools on their own in places like Kundapur, Hangarakatte, Brahnavar, Malpe and Tonse.

Industrial training centres were also started to give the boys some background of working in industrial units or alternatively become self-employed as carpenters or in other skilled and semi-skilled jobs.

Koragas were the poorest of the poor, but with education, they became aware of the world around them. And, over time, they were better assimilated

Kudmul-pijja established a residential school at Shedigudde especially for children who were from remote villages in the district. With the help of the government, Kudmul-pijja was able to run a school up to standard eight at there. Panchnama girls had their own separate school in Shedigudde. The school provided skill development to help the girls earn a living and lead a decent life without being dependent on others.

Kudmul-pijja also started an ashram for vulnerable women and child widows.

Chapter 20

Distribution of Lands to the Panchnamas

In the early days when Kudmul-pijja initiated reform in the society, he focused mainly on the Scheduled castes and Scheduled tribes who were entangled in the mire of social problems, suffered helplessly and were forbidden from entering society. The downtrodden had become prey to the bonded labour system, which came into existence because of the exploitation and domination of the upper castes who were wealthy landowners. Since there was no mobility between the classes and castes were hereditary there was not much scope for upward movement.

Over the years, Kudmul-pijja made sure that government lands were distributed to people belonging to the Koraga community in places like Udupi and Puttur. Wells were dug near their homes and he appealed to rich landlords – rather like Vinobha Bhave did in later times – to share their land with Koraga families. At Shedigudde, ten Koraga families were settled and provided with financial assistance to make a living using their skills in the crafts in which they were competent. He also ensured that the Mangalore Municipality employed the Koragas as sanitary workers.

A large part of the Harijan community lived in the Kapikadu area of Mangalore, so Kudmul-pijja built a beautiful building there. It was used for community activities like bhajans, prayers, public meetings, and social and cultural activities, which were organized every Saturday.

Close to the hall, there was a natural waterfall; Kudmul-pijja would take the gathering there so they could have a bath before praying. He encouraged group prayers in these meetings where he tried to explain the importance of unity and brotherhood. He also taught them the Gayatri Mantra, which was another point of contention.

How much of his teaching was absorbed by the listeners is a moot point. People were reluctant to change their habits and way of living.

Kudmul Ranga Rao, through his work for the depressed classes, became a household name among the Panchnamas. He is remembered with gratitude and venerated to this day.

The then British government also recognised the merit in his work and honoured him with the title of Rao Saheb, but since he did not crave honours and fame, he never flaunted this title. In fact, he used to joke that the only title he wanted was 'F.O.L.' or 'Father Of Lalitha.'

The collector of the district, Khan Bahadur M. Azizuddin Saheb, offered Kudmul-pijja some acres of land for his residents at Bijay. It is thought to have been ten acres of excellent land but he declined his offer with thanks.

Obviously, Kudmul-pijja was not greedy or acquisitive for large properties nor did houses attract him. He also did not want to be misunderstood by the public who would say that he had misappropriated land intended for Dalit colonies for his own use and for his own financial benefit.

The next collector, R. A. Graham, also promised him land in Mangalore that would be earmarked for the use of the Panchnamas. Kudmul-pijja declined this offer too.

However, his refusal to take land may have been a mistake. If he had accepted at least ten acres within five miles of Mangalore he would have had no difficulty in carrying on his work.

Kudmul-pijja moved among all classes of people. He talked to everybody, trying to get them interested in his ambition for the elevation of depressed classes. And several people responded positively and generously. For example, in suburban villages of Mangalore as far as Gurpur and Udupi, Dr Benegal Raghvendra Rao and Dr Keshav Pai gifted several acres of land on the condition that the lands were to be used to benefit Panchnamas. Even Kudmul-pijja's unmarried brother, Sadashiv Rao, donated his share of the family property.

DCM improved these grounds in several ways, including building sheds as residences for the local Panchnama.

Kudmul-pijja had either bought land outright to distribute or he used a system that is very peculiar to South Kanara alone and is still used.

There were landlords who had extensive lands that they used to lease out to tillers and farmers. These lands were leased out under the *Mulgeni* tenure or the *Chalgeni* tenure. The Mulgeni system meant the land belonged to the landowner but was 'rented' to the tenant with certain rights. This tenancy was largely hereditary, although naturally, these lands could not be sold without the consent of the original owner of the land. Chalgeni also gave tenure but without hereditary rights.

Kudmul-pijja purchased and was also gifted many acres of land from rich landlords in Daddalkad, Bijay Kapikadu colony and not to forget a few acres from a Muslim landlord from Kerala, which he took on lease and then distributed to the depressed classes for construction of houses and for farming.

He also purchased lands from the government in the villages of Koddelu, Udupi and Puttur for the Koraga community. Some parts of Kapikadu colony of Mangalore were taken for lease from Nellikayi Venkatraju and were distributed to the depressed castes.

Kudmul-pijja enforced certain restrictions on the distributed lands gifted to these people. They could not sell this land to other castes of the society, sales could only be transacted among themselves. Even to do this, they had to take prior permission from the DCM.

Main doors were constructed to the colonies and were locked during the nights. Even government officials, police and others had to take prior permission from the DCM to enter the premises at night. This system was implemented to make sure there were no distractions and make it easier for the inhabitants to lead a disciplined life.

At Derbil and Bijjal, the government was persuaded to have the land assessed at a low value for tax purposes to encourage them to build houses for themselves. The material for the houses like timber was supplied free, the plots were marked for each one of them from the several acres which were assessed. Wells were dug for drinking water. The only condition was they were not allowed to cancel debts by selling these properties for personal use.

Kudmul-pijja realized that the very act of ownership of any asset always creates a sense of security and permanency for the owner. That a landowner will think twice before jeopardising his position. Owning land generally makes people feel more settled and less inclined to risk losing it. This in turn brings awareness for intellectual and social growth.

In yet another measure, using his own money, Kudmul-pijja started a Provident Fund for 2000 rupees. The idea was to teach the Panchnamas to be thrifty and save their money for contingencies in the case of illness and death. The fund worked for some time but had to be closed for lack of funds.

Kudmul-pijja's ambitions grew and expanded to acquire more land for distribution in the villages of Bannanje, Udyavara, Padambur, Tanneerubavi and Bikampadi. He encouraged the Panchnama to build houses for themselves. He also acquired government land at Babu Gudde in Mangalore and built a school there. More work was undertaken in Udupi, Udyavara, Nejaru, Brahmavar, Puttur and Mulki.

Kudmul-pijja, through all these measures, not only brought hope and ambition among the people but also social awareness and the recognition for the need to organise and educate themselves.

Chapter 21

Bonded Labour

Bonded labour was an accepted way of life at the time. It was a system where rich landlords literally owned the Panchnamas, body and soul. Kudmul-pijja thought deeply about how he could help these Scheduled castes and Scheduled tribes to shake off all these social shackles of constant exploitation and miseries of poverty.

Kudmul-pijja worked out a campaign to train the Untouchables in their handicrafts, cottage industries, farming and growing of vegetables. His idea was that they could be offered ownership of the land and small houses as an incentive.

Chapter 22

Reservations for the Depressed Castes in Local Institutions

In Kudmul-pijja's day, there were no reservations for the Scheduled castes and Scheduled tribes in the District Board and Municipal Council of Mangalore. However, in 1888, the Dalit community in South Kanara – due to the efforts of one man, Kudmul Ranga Rao – had organised a protest demanding inclusion of the members of the Dalit community in the municipality.

As a result of this initiative, Kudmul-pijja's favourite teacher, Sri Angara Master, was appointed as the member of the District Board. The famous teacher of Udupi's Puttur colony, Sri Govinda Master was appointed as the representative of Scheduled castes and Scheduled tribes in the Municipal Council of Mangalore. As a first, two young Dalit men – Angara master and Govinda master – becoming members of the municipality. Thus, due to Kudmul-pijja's efforts, the Scheduled castes and the Scheduled tribes got the right to fair representation.

Kudmul-pijja believed that cooperation among the depressed classes was essential to make them economically strong. To achieve this, Kudmul-pijja put in Rs.2000 of his own money and established a cooperative society based on the principle of 'self-help.' Unfortunately, the society only functioned for a short time; it closed down far too soon due to lack of funds.

To understand the importance of what Kudmul-pijja did for the Dalits is to remember that Dr Ambedkar, the principal architect of our constitution, was born in 1891 in Mhow, Madhya Pradesh.

Chapter 23

Women's Empowerment and Upliftment

In Kudmul-pijja's times, women were treated like chattel or property. They were at the complete mercy of men. Child widows and unmarried women were treated with casual cruelty – like slaves or Untouchables.

At weddings, widows and destitute women were treated just like Mhars and Koragars. They were only allowed to eat leftovers. They were not allowed to eat the food cooked for the other guests but had to eat whatever was left on the plantain leaves. They were not allowed to drink water from the same vessels nor were they allowed to enter the houses of upper caste. To destroy their dignity and humiliate them further, these unfortunate women were not allowed to cover themselves from the waist up. They had to leave their torsos bare. They could only use the cloth to cover themselves up from their waist down.

In fact, widows were made to feel inferior in every way.

Kudmul-pijja actively encouraged women to carry on with their lives in spite of their past misfortunes. He travelled all over South Kanara trying to convince women to cover themselves with loose blouses. He had to assure them that there would be no bad luck from the curses or persecution from the higher caste would not harm or affect them.

He also used to implore higher caste Hindus not to waste the food on festive occasions so that neither Dalits nor women need be forced to eat leftovers.

Kudmul-pijja also encouraged post-puberty widow and inter-caste marriages.

And he practised what he preached. The first inter-caste marriage in Mangalore took place in 1911 when his second daughter, Radhabai, married Dr Subbarayan, who was a Mudaliar and thus a lower caste than the Saraswats.

The first widow remarriage was when he almost kidnapped, with the consent of a very near relative, a young widow of the Saraswat community way back in 1898 or 1899. He arranged her marriage to a Saraswat bachelor named Shreshta. The marriage was performed in the home of Sir Narayan Chandavarkar, Judge of the Bombay High Court and Vice Chancellor of Bombay University. The bride was given away by Mrs Chandavarkar.

Kudmul-pijja also worked towards the education of widows and the rehabilitation of destitute women in society. There were many cases where he took in women who did not have the resources to educate themselves. He opened schools where education was provided to women free of cost. He also built orphanages where all the inmates were widows. Outcastes from society, these unfortunate women were given protection and trained in jobs.

Naturally, Kudmul-pijja allowed no distinction between caste, creed and religion.

Along with their mothers, the children were taught income-generating skills like embroidery, weaving and basket-making. He aimed at empowering these women and their children to stand on their own two feet with their own earnings.

Kudmul-pijja also tried to arrange marriages for women who had been abandoned by their husbands. He kept dossiers on these young women and if they were of marriageable age he would try to arrange matrimonial alliances for them. Kudmul-pijja also maintained a regular register with statistics of the number of widows left unmarried. He became what amounted to a one-man marriage bureau.

When Kudmul-pijja heard of child widows or destitute women abandoned by their husbands, he would go out of his way to help. He would put in advertisements in newspapers inviting marriage proposals for these unhappy women. Further, his house was always open for those who could not find a place for the celebration of inter-caste marriages.

There were several cases where he ensured widows were remarried or inter-caste marriages happened. In one case, Kudmul-pijja sent a destitute Sudra girl to Bombay in the company of Bhai Baldev, a missionary of the Brahmo Samaj. He bore her expenses until she passed her matriculation examination from the University of Bombay. She later married a professor of English.

Unfortunately, his dream of building a separate school for destitute women and child widows could not be fulfilled in his lifetime. But after his death, with the efforts of a famous doctor, Dr Benegal Raghavendra Rao and the generous donations received from the public, 'Swami Ishwaranand Sevashram For Women' was constructed in the memory of Kudmul-pijja at Mangalore. Later on, Kudmul-pijja's two grandsons, Nyampalli Rama Rao and Nyampalli Shiva Rao, gifted land to shift this refugee home to Kankanadi Kudkorigudde.

Chapter 24
Fighting the Devadasi System

There was perfect harmony between Ullal Raghunathaiah and Kudmul-pijja in many of their fields of work. Their work in fighting the Daevadasi system was one of them. In those days, poor people sold their girl children to temples when they were as young as three years, where they were trained to be Devadasis.

These Devadasis were brought out on most religious occasions like Upanayanams, weddings, thread ceremonies and naming ceremonies to be used by men from the upper castes, including Saraswats, who could afford the fee.

The Muktis of temples actively encouraged this practice because the upper caste man paid large monies for the sexual abuse of these girls and the funds were used to augment temple funds.

Kudmul-pijja started an anti-nautch girl movement. He printed and published pamphlets and flyers condemning the practice. He also delivered speeches and lectures condemning the practice and encouraging men not to use these women for their pleasure.

However, the Devadasi system was pernicious and evil and his efforts were only partly successful. Still, thanks to his work these practices did stop for a while; however, they most certainly continued secretly in certain temples.

Sadly, this evil practice continues to this day. Efforts are still being made by the government to stop this exploitation of young girls.

Chapter 25
Rehabilitation of Prisoners

At one point in time, Kudmul-pijja was appointed the Honorary Magistrate of the area around Mangalore. Part of his duties involved visits to the jail whenever he felt the need to go.

On his trips there, he found some of the inmates had fallen victim to alcohol and that they were mostly Roman Catholics. On discovering this, he wrote to the Head of the Catholic Church that the evils of alcohol were proving to be a curse for the otherwise industrious community of Roman Catholics. He felt that these hapless people should be guided and counselled by the clergy.

This invoked the ire of the higher echelons of the Church. Some clergymen and prominent local Roman Catholics took offence and questioned his intentions, asking why he was insulting the Catholic community.

But Kudmul-pijja knew he could prove his point from the records of the Benoly court. So, he met the Bishop and told him that he felt great anguish for the community. His letter was meant not to insult or hurt the community's sentiments but to heal a social illness. Then, he presented a paper he had written where he supported his arguments with facts and figures.

This explanation satisfied Bishop who realised that Kudmul-pijja had no secret agenda.

Kudmul-pijja's visits to the jail were not merely formal. He used to try and help inmates to see that things could be done differently in a way which would enable them to lead better lives.

He used to question them about their ideas of God. He would ask them what they meant when they said they adored Him.

He wanted to create a thirst in them to make a better life for themselves, to rise above the lowest rung of society and plant within them a yearning and ardent desire and ambition for a better life.

The demon of drink had to be exorcised. He would call them to attend the meetings and used all his influence to try and persuade them and to wean them away from the evil of alcohol, which was the root of all their misery. In the same way as he did for the Dalits, he appealed to the authorities to give the Catholics sites free from taxes for building residences. This was once again done with an idea of creating in them a sense of self-respect and ownership.

Kudmul-pijja also started an organisation in which representatives from all religions were invited to become members. The idea was to collect contributions and subscriptions. With the money collected, Kudmul-pijja was able to build schools for their children. The fact that he was an Honorary Magistrate of the court for a long time helped in this endeavour.

Chapter 26
Financial Problems and Fund Raisers

Doing social service is not an easy or a glamorous task; money is scarce, the demands are heavy and every bit of money has to be saved. When Kudmul-pijja was running the hostels, there were nights he could not sleep as there was just enough rice in the storeroom for the morning meals. Further, his credit was limited as the upper classes did not like the work he was doing and they were happy to see that he was finding it difficult.

Things have changed since then, but 90 years ago when Kudmul-pijja started working, nobody even thought that untouchability, alcoholism, the Devadasi system, the ill-treatment of widows and other issues he tried to address were issues that needed to be thought of, let alone dealt with. Whereas Kudmul-pijja thought they were a cancer in society that needed to be removed.

Very often, Kudmul-pijja was overwhelmed with anxiety because there was no money to feed the children and his only recourse was appeal to the Almighty. Being an ardent believer, he felt He would provide.

He was not wrong. In times of need, provisions would arrive no one knew from where.

Surprisingly, he also got financial help from people who had heard of his work but never seen him. Reverend Justin Abbot was an American missionary who contributed Rs.50 annually until his death. In his will, he specifically left 1000 dollars for the DCM Mission.

Besides Reverend Abbot, there were others like Benegal Ramakrishna Rao, the Chief Medical officer in Baroda, who willed Rs 4000, which was received in 1930.

Mrs Narayana Rao, widow of the late Mr Narayan Rao, a financier from Bombay and a close friend of Kudmul-pijja, sent Rs 2500 as an endowment to the DCM.

These two endowments by Reverend Justin Abbot and Mrs Narayana Rao were received in 1930 after Kudmul-pijja had passed away.

The money received from Benegal Sadashiv Rao was used for the construction of the orphanage and boarding house in his memory.

In addition to these endowments, there were several others ranging from Rs.100 to Rs.500, which arrived for many years.

Kudmul-pijja also received a regular sum from the Venkatiah Trust. The trust also contributed towards the digging of a well in the school premises at Valencia, known as Ludmilla, which the owner, a Catholic gentleman, named after his foster granddaughter.

Mr Whitworth I.C.S., when in service, sent Kudmul-pijja Rs. 30 annually. After retirement, when he went to England, he did not forget Kudmul-pijja's work and in his will, he left Rs. 500 for the DCM.

Even Henry Ford, the manufacturer of Ford cars, seems to have heard of him and sent him money.

It is amazing to wonder how word of his work spread to other countries considering these were days before the advent of television, the internet or the mobile phone.

People who had not even visited Mangalore used to contribute regularly and unasked.

All these sums added up to help Kudmul-pijja in his mission.

Once the Mission faced an acute financial crisis. Kudmul-pijja had run out of funds. It was difficult to provide even food and basic facilities. He spent anxious days worrying about money but always remembered to correspond with friends who contributed after his letters of appeal. Contributions from them on occasions of bestowing of titles, birthdays, New year honours, marriages were all opportunities asking for their help. He raised funds both with his tongue and pen.

Kudmul-pijja used to tell his students to post his letters of appeal with a prayer. It seems that God always heard him.

In crucial periods when there was no food to feed the children, Kudmul-pijja would go from house to house, carrying a bag asking for rice, coconuts and other needs to feed the children.

Fortunately, social activists like Sri Mundappa Bangera and Sri Narasappaiah stepped up and supported him financially. This enabled him to carry on with his work.

Kudmul-pijja also made an effort to find out the names of the most generous donors of the organization. Once, on checking the list, he found the name of a British industrialist, a Mr Morgan. As soon as that his name came up, he called Sri Ekambara Rao, the secretary of the DCM, and asked him to write a letter to Mr Morgan, describing the situation and the desperate need for help, ending with a request for some money.

At the time, Sri Ekambara Rao was a fresh graduate, who worked as a teacher in Ganapathy High School and also as the honorary secretary of DCM. He did as requested and the letter was sent through Udupi Kunjibettu Gopala Krishna Master, an untouchable.

On reading the contents of the letter, Mr Morgan was furious and threw the letter away. He shouted at Gopala Krishna Master and ordered him to leave the place immediately.

Gopala Krishna Master took the letter, trembling with fear, and returned it to Kudmul-pijja and related the incident directly to him.

Kudmul-pijja was horrified to see that the young and inexperienced Sri Ekambara Rao had written the letter in the form of an order and not as a request. So, on the back of the same letter, he wrote another letter, first apologizing, then seeking monetary help in a simple and humble manner. He sent it back with Gopala Krishna Master.

On reading the letter, the British Lord went inside his bungalow, opened the cupboard and brought out silver coins, tied them in a cloth to make a big bundle, gave it to Gopala Krishna Master and asked him to carefully hand it over to Kudmul-pijja.

Kudmul-pijja was always ready to acknowledge a mistake and did not feel a lesser person for having to apologise and explain his lapse.

News of Kudmul-pijja's efforts to help the less fortunate resonated abroad as well. He used to receive letters from great personalities expressing their respect, goodwill and appreciation. Some of them donated money, but others sent their contribution in the form of books. With these donations, the DCM library became well known for its valuable collection of books. The gift of books was appreciated because Kudmul-pijja loved books and was a voracious reader.

The British governors and dignitaries who came to Mangalore would always visit DCM. There were many people of renown like Rabindranath Tagore, Charles Freer Andrews, whom Gandhiji called Deenabandhu, or "Friend of the Poor," and Dr Annie Besant. Later, Mahatma Gandhi also made a trip to DCM. Shri Gopalakrishna Gohkle, the founder of Servants of India Society, the social reformer from North Karnataka, Sriman Thakkar Bapha, G.K Devdhar, the Right Honourable Srinivasa Sastri were all Kudmul-pijja's admirers and friends.

After all these great men came to Mangalore, Kudmul-pijja corresponded with them. Unfortunately, these are among the letters that were lost along with the papers that were given to the paper-wallah.

Chapter 27
Handing Over the Reins

By 1923, Kudmul-pijja had become quite frail and was keeping indifferent health. So, although he was still guiding the institutions he had founded, he knew he had to give it up. So Kudmul-pijja wrote to the Right Honourable V.S. Sastriar of the Servants of India Society requesting him to take over the institutions being run by the DCM.

The Servants of the India society (Bharata Sevaka Sangha) was founded in Pune, Maharastra, in 1905 by Gopal Krishna Gokhale. Along with him were a small group of educated Indians like Natesh Appaji Dravid, Gopal Krishna Deodhar and Anant Patwardhan. The society was formed to promote social and human development in India. They were involved in education, sanitation, health care and fought the social evils of untouchability and discrimination, alcoholism, poverty, oppression of women and domestic abuse.

The society chose to remain away from political activities and organizations like the Indian National Congress and its base shrank after Gokhale's death in 1915 and in the 1920s with the rise of Mahatma Gandhi, who launched social reform campaigns on a far larger and more national scale, which attracted young Indians to the cause. By 1923, the Servants of India was a smaller, albeit still a fairly well-known organisation all over India for its work, which they conducted with compassion and integrity. And for the many young educated people who had joined it to dedicate their lives to philanthropic work.

Kudmul-pijja must have known that the society campaigned against the same ills that he had. He would have known that the Servants of India Society and DCM shared common objectives, so his life's work would be in good hands.

Today, the society still continues its activities and has a small membership. Its headquarters are in the city of Pune, Maharashtra and it has branches in various other states. It still runs primary schools, residential hostels for tribal boys, ashram type schools for tribal girls, creche centres and other initiatives that impact society.

However, in 1953 after Independence, DCM, its properties and goodwill were handed over to the Government of Madras.

DCM was the institution that particularly interested Gandhiji. He wanted to visit it when he came to Mangalore in 1932.

It took almost 30 years for Kudmul-pijja's struggle to bear fruit. In those three decades, he not only started schools, he also started vocational training centres. He encouraged cottage industries. He worked on widow rehabilitation and remarriage. He worked against the Devadasi system. Most of all, he worked to improve the lot of the lower castes.

The Panchnamas in the Kanaras benefited hugely from all these efforts and they made a huge difference to their lives. But today, Kudmul-pijja would most certainly be proud to see that the difference between castes in South Kanara is virtually non-existent, particularly among the younger generation.

THE END OF AN
HONOURABLE LIFE

Chapter 28

Sanyasa

In Hinduism, there are four stages of life starting with 'Brahmacharya' when a child is expected to live at a Gurukula where he spends his time with his Guru. It is a period of learning.

The next stage is the 'Grihastha' where the man joins the world, gets married, has a family and stays as a Grihastha till he finishes all his responsibilities.

When he feels that all he can do in the world has been accomplished he goes through a stage of 'Vanaprastha' where he goes into the forest living a very simple life dedicated to prayer.

Lastly, he takes to 'Sanyasa' which is considered the final stage of the ashrama systems and is traditionally taken by men or women at or beyond the age of fifty years or by young monks who wish to renounce worldly and materialistic pursuits and instead dedicate their entire life towards spiritual pursuits.

This was a widely followed pattern. Even earthly sovereigns, who ruled large empires, abdicated their thrones in favour of their descendants and retired to live the life of hermits. In the regulation of the worldly conduct of a householder, the maxim was laid down that all the desires and ambition for power or wealth should have as their ultimate aim spiritual freedom, which is well expressed in the formula *Dharma (Nature) Artha (Truth) Kama (Desire) Moksha (Release from desire)*.

It was considered the duty of the wealthy to build temples, big tanks, construct choultries and washing places for the hungry and the thirsty.

There are passages in Hindu religious texts or the *Puranas* and historical tracts known as *Itihasas* where poverty is extolled and riches condemned.

From the time of his childhood in his village of Kudmul, Kudmul-pijja had been a great devotee of the Almighty. He not only always started each day with a prayer in the morning, apparently he was truly responsive to the faint whispers of the Supreme Spirit. As his soul expanded in the sphere of his work, he saw the Divine in each and every individual. There were very little of the self which merged with the Divine.

He was unaware of all his creature comforts, uncaring about his belongings and never thought of the welfare of himself and his family. He completely identified himself with the causes he espoused and devoted intense concentration to the tasks he set himself. No doubt he lived in this world but he was above its temptations. Nor did he mind the troubles and difficulties, the harassment and the discomforts that he had to face while carrying out his work. He worked in absolute self-abandonment.

Like *The Gita* prescribes, he cultivated the spirit of detachment.

However, once he handed over the management of all his institutions to the Servants of Indian Society, he lost interest in an active social life.

Kudmul-pijja was a devotee of the Almighty but not at all taken in by the rites and rituals. However, to those who knew him, it was not surprising that towards the closing years of his life, when he could no longer work, he thought of ending his days in contemplation of the Divine Spirit. His decision to take on Sanyasa was but a fitting and appropriate step at the end of an active life in service of the Divine. We can be sure that he meditated deeply for a long time before he took this step.

This decision changed the rest of his life.

In 1924, it was arranged that Maharshi Shraddananda, the disciple of Dayananda Saraswati, would come to Mangalore for a second time for the inauguration function of the Arya Samaj.

The Arya Samaj is an Indian Hindu reform movement that promotes values and practices based on the belief in the infallible authority of *The Vedas*. The Samaj was founded by the Sanyasi Dayananda Saraswati on 10 April 1875. Members of the Arya Samaj believe in one God and reject the worship of idols.

Kudmul-pijja decided to take Sanyasa from Shraddananda Swamiji but this desire was not fulfilled because someone murdered the Sanyasi at Delhi station.

But Kudmul-pijja's decision was firm.

Finally, in 1927, he took Sanyasa in Thrissur from Ganapath Rao, a Gowd Saraswat who later on life became a disciple of Shraddananda Swamiji and an ascetic and took the name of Swami Suvicharananda.

He was given the name 'Ishwarananda Swamiji' from Vidya Vachaspathi and took on the mantle of a Sanyasi, carrying a *Danda (stick)* and *Kamandulu* (this is an oblong water pot made of a dry gourd or coconut shell, metal, or the wood of the Kamandalataru tree, or from clay, usually with a handle and sometimes with a spout).

The other Brahmins thought he had reverted back to Hinduism because he had taken Sanyasa which, people averred, was more Hindu than Brahmo.

As was his wont, Kudmul-pijja had kept his decision to himself and had told nobody about his decision to take Sanyasa. So nobody knew that he had been given *Diksha* (initiation) until the moment he stepped down from the train in Mangalore with his *Kavevastra* (this is the Konkani word for the saffron clothes worn by sanyasis and the act of becoming a Sanyasi).

Kudmul-pijja took his vows seriously and spent most of his time in prayer, meditation and reading the scriptures. At this stage, he must have felt that he had disentangled himself from the pulls of worldly affairs.

He was a simple man, N. Rama Rao, his grandson, used to tell his children, nieces and nephews. On the way to the renunciation, Kudmul-pijja apparently told Rama Rao, "I have worn my best clothes of silk which I will have to change to Kavevastra." He immediately he realised what he had said and laughed, "Look how foolish I am! I am taking Sanyasa and I'm worried about my silk clothes!"

This renunciation, he genuinely believed, relieved him from attachments of worldly attractions. He even came to see the titles the government had bestowed on him as impediments to the cultivation of the spirit. He thought they hindered the progress of directing the mind towards its true goal. When he took the vow of Sanyasa and was ordained as Swami Isharwarananda Swami, one of the offerings he made to Agni, the God of fire, was the title of Rao Saheb and all his other honours and certificate.

The only title he wanted for himself was that of a Sanyasi.

It is tempting to want wealth and honour and not too difficult to acquire it. But to give it up and turn your back on all that fame and comfort that comes from being born into a higher caste in those days could not have been easy.

Kudmul-pijja owned the house he lived in along with the surrounding land. It is on the street that is now called Kudmul Ranga Rao Road. However, he donated all this to the ashram leaving him destitute towards the end of his life. He could leave nothing for his family.

As a Sanyasi, he moved to his daughter's house in Shiv Bagh, so, towards the end of his life, Kudmul-pijja had his family around him. But he didn't stay in Shiv Bagh, the main house. Instead, he occupied a small home with black flooring and wooden beams below the main house. This was where the *Machu*, or domestic help, stayed later on. It was a pleasant place, surrounded by fruit trees and a well for their needs. His grandson, Rama Rao, referred to it as the *Thogu Ghara* (lower-level house in Konkani) and he used to visit Kudmul-pijja there almost every day.

Nor was he the only visitor. Kudmul-pijja had a great sense of humour, a wide range of interests and was a great conversationalist, so he had many visitors even after he had retired.

After Kudmul-pijja took Sanyasa he knew he was supposed to have no desires. But, one day he called his grandson, Rama Rao, and said, "Ramarai, a Sanyasi is supposed to have no desires, but I have this tremendous desire to see Sadhu Vaswani."

Sadhu T.L Vaswani was then Thanwardas Likram Vaswani. He had originally set up his mission in Hyderabad, Sindh, now in Pakistan, but then moved to Pune, India.

Rama Rao tried to find a way to make this meeting possible, but it was not to be because Kudmul-pijja passed away three days later. However, at his 13th-day ceremony, without any notice, without anyone seeing him, without an invitation or even the knowledge of his family, Sadhu Vaswani attended the function, said a few words and left without making too much of an issue about it.

Chapter 29

Death

Kudmul-pijja had only one selfish request to make to the Almighty. He did not want a long and protracted illness through which he would inflict suffering on his near and dear ones. He wanted a quick death although he did not mind any pain personally.

The Almighty obliged, and he suffered only for about an hour. It was a case of coronary thrombosis.

Apparently, he uttered, "Narayan, Narayan, Narayan!" loudly at first and when the end came it was just another, "Narayan!" a little louder, for he had met his Maker.

His eldest grandson, N Rama Rao, was witness to this, as he was sitting by Kudmul-pijja when he breathed his last.

Kudmul Ranga Rao died on the 30th of January 1928 when he was 69 years old. It was the auspicious day of Bhishma Janam Ashtami, the day on which we remember the great grandfather in *The Mahabharata*.

Coincidentally, two decades later, Gandhi was also assassinated on the same date, 30th January 1948.

In accordance with his beliefs, Kudmul-pijja did not leave much to his children in terms of material wealth. He left behind a small house in Kadri, which he had donated to the ashram, but more importantly, he gave his children a good education. He also passed on his belief in total honesty and his convictions about equality and fair play to his children and grandchildren.

Towards the end of his life, having given away most of all he possessed, he was more or less destitute and had to move to his daughter's house. Not much is known about his wife. It seems that Rukmini-amma predeceased him.

Kudmul-pijja's passing away created a huge void. His death was a day of sorrow and grief to all, especially Dalits whom he had befriended and given hope for bettering their lives.

When the news spread, people from all over the district came to pay their last respects at the home of N. Subba Rao and Lalithabai.

Chapter 30

Funeral

January 30, 1928, the day Kudmul-pijja died, was six days after Rama Rao's daughter, Tara (later Chandavarkar) was born. So they couldn't have a Sath Devi Pooja which was the normal practice.

Still, Kudmul-pijja's caring, concern and deep-rooted feelings for the Panchnamas that he had helped in so many ways, was reflected in his will which he had written a few years before his death. His dream of uplifting the Thoti community, the traditional sanitary workers' community in Dakshina Kannada and Udupi, had not materialised. But when he died on January 30, 1928, his will stated that he wanted people belonging to the Thoti community to carry his body to the burial grounds. It was an apt reflection of the scant regard he had for social conventions. It also showed the level of his commitment, because even in death he made one last significant attempt to uplift that community.

When his will was read out, upper caste people were outraged and enraged. It was considered blasphemy for the Mhars and the Koragas to carry the body of a higher caste person to the crematorium or the burial ground. And the Thotis were the lowest of the low!

These attitudes were so ingrained in society that the upper caste Brahmins honestly believed that a body thus tainted by the Thotis would not go the Heaven but to eternal Hell and Perdition. It was considered to be the highest form of punishment because the higher castes believed that a soul of such a person would never find peace.

But Kudmul-pijja obviously considered this as the greatest possible reward for his life's deeds. He seemed to indicate that he preferred Hell if Heaven was a place where people were discriminated against because of their caste.

There seems to have been almost a riot in reaction to Kudmul-pijja's will and the crowd had to be pacified by his son-in-law N. Subba Rao. According to some reports, different communities carried the body for different distances, but others say that eventually the body was carried by the Thotis. Whatever the case, the point had been made one last time.

Lalithabai's memory of her father was written down. Since it is undated, it was probably read out at his memorial.

"KR Rao, with his work with the downtrodden and poor, became a household name in the Kanaras. He was almost worshipped among the Untouchables who revered and venerated him. The British government of that time conferred the title of Rai Saheb on him for his work and dedication.

"At the end of his life, the desolate Dalits could well have recited this poem by Shelley;

"'He has outsoar'd the shadow of our night;

"'Envy and calumny and hate and pain,

"'And that unrest which men miscall delight,

"'Can touch him not and torture not again.'"

Kudmul-pijja's tomb is in the compound of the Brahmo Samaj Mission House near Nandigudde in Mangalore. His *Asti* is buried there. It was in a shabby condition, so his grandson,

Kudmul Sadashiv Rao, collected money from all the family members and improved the premises.

Today, sociologists at Mangalore University attribute the wide social acceptance of the oppressed classes in Dakshina Kannada today to Kudmul-pijja's brave efforts. But what he would have undoubtedly considered more important is that thousands of families belonging to the so-called depressed classes in Dakshina Kannada and Udupi districts regard him as their saviour.

Kudmul-pijja is remembered to this day by the Panchnamas. They all come to pay silent homage to him on his anniversary. His tomb is decorated with flowers and prayers are recited.

Chapter 31
How Gandhiji was Inspired

As a part of the Freedom Movement, Gandhiji wanted to change the social status of the Untouchables who made up 1/5 of India's population. Gandhiji believed that it would be meaningless to attain Independence without the overall development of the Untouchables.

He proclaimed at many public meetings that attaining the independence of the country without the reformation of society cannot be called as independence in the real sense. The Untouchables had been treated as the outcasts of society and exploited for hundreds of years.

In fact, Gandhiji had lived with them in their colonies as their friend to understand their condition personally – exactly what Kudmul-pijja had done about 25 years earlier to know and feel the pain of these people.

In order to achieve this goal, Gandhiji travelled all over the country. He started a great social revolution against the basic problems of the depressed like poverty, untouchability, social injustice and other social problems. As a part of his revolution, Gandhiji visited Mangalore thrice.

On the eve of 24th February at 7 PM 1934, all the arrangements were made for Mahatma Gandhi's visit to DCM School at Shedigudde. The Panchnamas and other people started to arrive at the school. By the evening, there was a heavy rush and many could not enter the school building and had to remain outside.

At first, Gandhiji looked over the craftwork of the school children, the garden maintained by them and expressed his appreciation. Gandhiji was very impressed by service Kudmul-pijja had rendered through DCM. Gandhiji then addressed the gathering where a large number of Scheduled castes and Scheduled tribes had gathered. He said he considered the founder member of the DCM the 'ideal man.' Kudmul-pijja's service towards humanity and his vision had helped Gandhiji to understand the burdens the Panchnamas had to carry. In all sincerity, Gandhiji proclaimed that Kudmul-pijja was his 'guru' who had shown him the way to whole-heartedly undertake the cause of eradicating untouchability from society. Gandhiji stated that not only did he admire Kudmul-pijja's movement but that he had taken inspiration from it.

Gandhiji advised the students to be appreciative of the privileges they had received from the DCM. He reminded them that they, in turn, should give back in good measure to society what they had received. He was full of praise for DCM as it was the oldest institution in India doing this kind of work. He proclaimed that all institutions working for the depressed members of the society should follow the example set by the school.

In many ways, this vindicated Kudmul-pijja's hard work for the upliftment of society.

Of course, by then, Kudmul-pijja was no more. But one of the members of the extended family, Vasanti Chandavarkar, remembers being taken to the maidan for the public meeting and Gandhiji standing on a stage and her excitement at being able to sit at the foot of the podium.

Chapter 32
Kudmul-Pijja's Work Continued

Kudmul-pijja did not have the capital to start new ashrams and homes with his own resources. All he had had was his home in Kadri which he donated.

However, after his death, many institutions were started in his memory.

The Ishwarananda Mahila Seva Ashram Society was started in 1928. It was opened in front of the Bundt Hostel in Mangalore by Doctor Benegal Raghvendra Rao and a team of dedicated people. It was planned to support destitute helpless women and children with no discrimination with regard to caste or creed. The aim was to make the women self-supporting and self-reliant.

The society now maintains Balika Ashrama, an educational boarding ashram for girls from five and a half years. It also houses cottages for destitute children ranging from five and a half to 18 years of age. This is all part of an educational and boarding ashram, which educates these children up to SSLC or PUC.

Finally, the society runs a working women's hostel. The donations of 3.5 acres of land at Kankaady, on which these buildings are grouped, was made by the Late Sri Nyampalli Rama Rao and Sri Nyampalli Shiva Rao in 1956. Of this 1.25 acres was later acquired by the government for a bypass for which compensation was paid. The society owes its growth mainly to the generosity of the Nyampalli brothers who donated the land in memory of their grandfather, Kudmul Ranga Rao.

This is an extract of the gift deed:

"This deed of gift by (1) Nyampalli Rama Rao, son of Diwan Bahadur N. Subha Rao, Landholder, residing at Mercara Hill, Mangalore and (2) Nyampalli Shiva Rao, Son of Diwan Bahadur N Subha Rao, Director of Imperial Tobacco Company Ltd., Calcutta, now come to Mangalore hereinafter collectively called the donors in favour of the Ishwarananda Mahila Seva Ashram, a society registered under the Societies Registration Act with its office in Mangalore represented by its Honorary Secretary, hereinafter called the Donee.

"Whereas the donors and their elders have been intimately associated with the Donee Institution and have been encouraging social advancement of the people and whereas the late Swamy Ishwarananda, after whom the Ishwarananda Mahila Seva Ashram is named, did yeomen service in the cause of advancement and amelioration of destitute children and discarded wives, and whereas the ashram has worked successfully all these years for the purposes for which the society has been incorporated."

Chapter 33
Looking Back

A hundred and odd years later when we look back, we cannot help but admire Kudmul-pijja's courage and determination. He took on a society that had such deeply entrenched ideas, motivated only by his revulsion for the state of affairs that deprived Dalits of a decent life and the right to be treated like human beings instead of animals.

Then there were issues like education for all, the allotment of land for the construction of houses for the underprivileged, child widow remarriage, employment, the development of financial security – we might well ask how these ideas occurred to him.

It was not something that was passed down by his family, society or community. It was entirely his own foresight and vision.

As the saying goes, when you reach rock bottom the only way to move is upward and there will always be a hand to lift you. God seems to have appointed Kudmul-pijja to provide that hand to the Panchnamas.

As has been proved time and time again, economic, social and educational developmental of any exploited people can only be through education. They should also be able to lead a respectable life and not fall prey to the dominant members of the society or oppressed by the upper castes. They should get a fair price for their handicrafts and their handicrafts and cottage industries should be developed. Kudmul-pijja had even planned to establish model industrial units.

His vision was that the socially depressed should lead an independent, self-reliant and respectable life in society and not let the upper classes impose their power on them due to an accident of birth.

It was not easy to fulfil the aims and commitments he had envisaged. On one hand, there was constant opposition from the orthodox upper castes and his own friends and relatives. Their opposition was so virulent that he had been excommunicated from his own Saraswat community. And on the other hand, there was the intransigence of the Panchnamas themselves.

Even so under these circumstances to achieve his goals, Kudmul-pijja stood firm with determination and courage against all odds. All this with a smile and sense of humour.

There is a big difference now in the status of the Dalits in South Kanara. There is a feeling that they too have a place under the sun and they that can take control of their lives, without fear of reprisals from other castes. This is an achievement in many respects due to the untiring efforts and commitment of one humble and sincere man who lived in the 19th and early 20th Century.

What was unique about Kudmul-pijja's work and thinking was how far ahead he was of his times. No one had even thought of the ideas brimming in his mind. In fact, his ideas of inclusion and education and treatment of women were unheard of and his endeavours ridiculed.

What was even more extraordinary was that his movement was not militant or aggressive. His achievements were a result of persuasion and personal example. He tried to change ideas through gentle means. His efforts were more to open people's mind to what was evil and inhuman in society and what changes could be made to make life better for fellow human beings.

Later on, what he tried to do at a local level was taken up by Gandhiji and Doctor Ambedkar at a national level. They also emulated Kudmul-pijja's methods of gentle persuasion and personal example.

Kudmul-pijja may be called a true Bhakta, a believer and a devotee of the Almighty. Such people do not need statues in their memory but what they will leave behind are memories of love and gratitude. Kudmul-pijja will always be enshrined in the hearts of those who knew him, his descendants and the thousands who benefited from his ideas and hard work.

True the huge achievements he had to his credit were limited to the Kanaras. But they showed that change was possible and could happen in a rigid society with numerous dos and don'ts. Kudmul-pijja espoused an ideology that was diametrically new and different from what existed then, and what had existed for millennia.

Of course, change could not be achieved overnight. But a seed had been planted which bloomed over the next century. His ideas and aspirations took root in the students of the school that was set up. They realised that education was the first step to achieve success and to break the shackles of the caste system. The values, aspirations and ambitions have changed the perspective of the Untouchables and have given them the courage to realise that democracy means equal opportunities and rights for all.

Further, women now can also come out and control their lives through education and skilled development that have allowed them financial security and independence.

Today, South Kanara can boast of at least a partial breakdown of the caste system with its rigidity and cruelty, although there is a long way to go. The way that the society in that part of the state works is proof that Kudmul-pijja did, at least partially, change the mindset of society and slowly turn the wheel of progress. He showed that if you believe in an idea and are willing to devote your life to it, change is possible. He did this and awakened people to make changes in their lifestyles.

Kudmul-pijja's achievements may seem minuscule compared to larger movements. However, it did break many taboos and allowed the underprivileged to have a glimpse of what they could hope for and achieve in this newly opened world.

As a little couplet tells us;

"Two prisoners looked out of prison bars,

"One saw mud, the other stars."

Kudmul-pijja worked hard for those aspiring for a better life and urged them to look towards the stars. The initial work and the thought of improving the conditions of Panchnamas and alleviating their poverty and improving their standards of education were his alone.

To quote from Denita UshaPrabha's research paper 2012: "As a great social reformer, he did everything for the well-being of the Untouchables at the cost of his family. His intervention in the life of the Untouchables in Dakshina Karnataka was a major event. There was a remarkable unity between his precepts and practice. He practised at the level of the locality a set of inclusionary practices, unique in their own way, which was one of the main tendencies at the national level too at that time. In KRR, the ideas of enlightenment and liberalism were joined with deep sensibility, about injustice and urge for social service, and a practical, active attitude of mind."

Kudmul-pijja once said, "When a Dalit community boy educated in my institution gets a good government job and travels in a car to my village and when the dust arises in the street by such a Dalit person moving in a car touches my head, then I will feel my life is worth living and I am fulfilled."

These words were later engraved on Kudmul-pijja's grave.

Today, the Dalit Community in the Kanaras can now boast of lawyers, doctors, IAS officers, teachers and fashion designers. There is almost a hundred percent literacy among the younger generation of both boys and girls. Even villages are well-integrated with all castes living in harmony.

Kudmul-pijja's dream has gone a long way towards being fulfilled in South Kanara albeit after a period of 90 years. This would most certainly have made him a happy and contented man.

References and Bibliography

Nyampalli Shiva Rao's (Grandson) speech on great Brahmo women.

Extracts from "Our Portraits Gallery."

Three saviours of the Dalits – 'Kudumul Ranga Rao – a chronicle of his life' by P Kamalaksha in 1986, printed at Srinidhi printers.

Lest we forget by N Rama Rao (Grandson) 29/6/1859 to 30/01/28

Lalithbai's (daughter) memories of K Ranga Rao.

Lalithabai's handwritten letter to her father from the Coronation Durbar in 1911.

Information shared by N Subba Shiva Rao (Great-grandson).

Memories of those days by Tara Chandavarkar (great-granddaughter).

Naming of City Corporation Hall by MCC as K Ranga Rao Hall.

Memorial speech by Tara Chandavarkar at N Shiva Rao's service 1976.

Article in Prajavani and other newspapers.

Spectrum August 18/2015. Notes on College and its famous alumni.

Apostle of Sacrifice – Deshbhakta K Sadashiva Rao compiled by Karnad Radha and Saguna Desai (daughters).

Reminiscences by Vasnthi Chandavarkar.

Speech by Tara Chandavarkar about Lalitha Bai and her father given in 1949. To quote "who realised God in the service of the poor, the weak and the downtrodden." Author unknown.

Thesis on K Ranga Rao by Usha Prabha.

History of the Ishwarananda Ashram and Home for women.

The Saraswats by B N Kuduva.

A gentle Life by Sita Shiva Rao (granddaughter in law).

In memory of KRR, Swamy Iswarananda Mahila Seva Ashram was opened in front of the Bundt Hostel in Mangalore by Doctor Benegal Raghvendra Rao. This was later shifted to Kankanady on the land donated by his two grandsons Nyampalli Rama Rao and Nyampalli Shiva Rao.